Reading Essentials® in Science

LIFE SCIENCE INVESTIGATIONS

How Plants Grow

HELEN LEPP FRIESEN

PERFECTION LEARNING®

T 100059

$18.95

Gumdrops

1 SEPT 06

Editorial Director: Susan C. Thies
Editor: Lori A. Meyer
Design Director: Randy Messer
Book Design: Robin Elwick, Emily J. Greazel
Cover Design: Michael A. Aspengren

A special thanks to the following for his scientific review of the book:
Paul J. Pistek, Instructor of Biological Sciences, Mason City, IA

Image Credits:

©Bettmann/CORBIS: p. 28 (bottom); ©Martin B. Withers/Frank Lane Picture Agency/
CORBIS: p. 20 (left); ©Richard Hamilton Smith/CORBIS: p. 25 (inset); ©Associated
Press: p. 27

©iStock International Inc.—©Arlene Gee: p. 5 (top); ©Joshua Sowin: p. 8 (left);
©Carol Gering: p. 23 (inset); ©Sang Nguyen: p. 24; ©Michel Mory: p. 26; Corel
Professional Photos: p. 5 (bottom); Emily J. Greazel: p. 14 (top), 21 (inset);
Michael A. Aspengren: pp. 19 (top), 20 (top right); Photos.com: pp. 3, 4, 6, 7, 8 (right),
9, 10, 11, 12, 13, 14 (bottom), 15, 16, 18 (right), 19 (bottom), 20 (bottom right),
21 (background), 22, 23 (background), 25 (background), 28 (top), 31; Robin Elwick:
pp. 17, 18 (left)

For information, contact
Perfection Learning® Corporation
1000 North Second Avenue, P.O. Box 500
Logan, Iowa 51546-0500.
Phone: 1-800-831-4190
Fax: 1-800-543-2745
perfectionlearning.com

1 2 3 4 5 6 PP 10 09 08 07 06 05

Paperback ISBN 0-7891-6635-6
Reinforced Library Binding ISBN 0-7569-4695-6

CONTENTS

1 PLANTS AND HOW THEY GROW

Take a look around outside and you may see many different plants. Some are tall with long graceful needles, like the majestic ponderosa pine. Others are short with round stubby leaves like an African violet. Some have flowers. Some bear fruit. Some are poisonous. Some need a lot of water, and others can survive with very little. Plants live in a wide variety of **habitats**. The combinations are almost endless. Come along on this plant quest and you will learn how plants grow.

The World of Plants

Did you know that there are more than 300,000 different kinds of plants on Earth? They play important roles in the environment. Plants beautify our world and provide us with food, shelter, clothing, medicine, and energy. Besides that, they keep nature in balance by providing us with fresh air to breathe.

Even though there are so many different kinds of plants, most are green and make their own food through

photosynthesis. Most plants also live in or on soil and do not move around by themselves, except when they grow.

Plants have varying life cycles. Some plants such as many garden vegetables complete their life cycle in one season. Then there are those plants like the giant sequoia that can live for thousands of years.

Cherry tomato plant

Tree Giants

Did you know that the largest trees on Earth live in the Sequoia National Forest in California? General Sherman and General Grant are two of the biggest trees. General Sherman is 272 feet high, has 3-foot-thick bark, and weighs more than 2000 tons. These giants are estimated to be between 1800 and 2700 years old.

Plants can be grouped into two categories based on whether they have flowers or not. Wildflowers, many trees, and most fruits and vegetables belong to the flowering plants. **Conifers**, ferns, and mosses belong to the nonflowering plants since they do not produce flowers.

Cosmos flowers (flowering)

Conifers (nonflowering)

Plant Reproduction

Both flowering and nonflowering plants grow in a similar way. Both groups must reproduce in order to continue the cycle of life. Since plants cannot move around, how can they accomplish this? They depend on and use many different methods to get the job done.

Pollination

Many plants' life cycles include **pollination**. This means that insects, animals, or the wind carry pollen to fertilize the female parts of the plant. A fertilized plant produces a seed that is capable of making a new plant.

Many plants such as grass, weeds, and even big pine trees depend on the wind for pollination. The wind picks up and easily carries the light pollen. The pollen lands on other plants to fertilize them.

Insects also pollinate plants. When a bee visits a flower to gather nectar, tiny grains of pollen stick to its hairy legs and body. When the bee moves on to the next flower, it takes the pollen with it. The pollen gets brushed off onto the female part of the flower.

Other animals help pollinate plants too. Birds such as hummingbirds and sunbirds and mammals such as bats and rodents assist in the pollination of plants.

Insects carry pollen.

A hummingbird helps with pollination.

Seeds

Have you ever picked a dandelion and blown on the white fluffy cluster? Did you know that you are helping to grow new dandelions? Plants depend on the wind and animals to scatter their seeds so they can keep on growing.

Dandelion

Seeds come in a wide variety of shapes, sizes, and packaging. Some are small and light and others are large and heavy. Many flowers' seeds are light and easily become **airborne,** while acorns and pinecones are too heavy for the wind to carry.

Sometimes animals carry seeds by eating the fruits of plants. When their digestive system expels the seeds, they are spread to other areas and new plants grow.

Bulbs

Plants also grow and reproduce from bulbs. The adult plant produces buds or bulbs. They split off and start to grow a new plant. Tulips and daffodils are examples of plants that reproduce and grow from bulbs.

Tulip bulbs

Roots

Certain plants start from just a root of an existing plant. A new raspberry plant will start from just a root.

Stems

Some new plants will grow from a stem of the main plant. Geraniums can grow like that. When you place the stem in water and keep it out of sunlight, roots will appear. The plant can then be planted in soil.

Venus Flytrap

A few unique plants are carnivorous. That means they feed on insects and other small animals, as well as produce food in their leaves. A common carnivorous plant is the Venus flytrap. Its leaves are traps in disguise. Sweet nectar on the lobes of the leaves attracts insects. When an insect touches the tiny hairs on the surface of the leaves, the two lobes snap shut. The insect gets trapped inside, and the plant uses enzymes to digest its prey. Because the Venus flytrap absorbs **nutrients** from insects, it is able to live in acidic, nutrient-poor soil where most other plants could not survive.

2 WHAT PLANTS NEED TO GROW

Just like you need air, water, food, and shelter to survive, plants also have specific needs. Most plants can grow both indoors and outdoors, but they need seven things to be able to grow well—air, light, water, nutrients, warmth, time, and space.

Fresh Air!

Plants need air. Plants use both oxygen and carbon dioxide.

You Light Up My Life!

Plants also need light to grow. Outdoor plants gather sunlight, and indoor plants get sunlight from windows or artificial light from lamps and lighting. You can tell when a plant isn't getting enough light. The leaves turn pale, and the stem gets thinner and leans toward the available light.

Inquire and Investigate: Plants and Sunlight

Question: What will happen to a plant leaf if it doesn't get sunlight?

Answer the question: I think a plant leaf without sunlight will

_____.

Form a hypothesis: A plant leaf will _____ without sunlight.

Test the hypothesis:

Materials:
- Any potted plant you have at home
  (ask first whether you can use the plant for an experiment)
- A piece of aluminum foil

Procedure:
1. Place the plant in a sunny spot.
2. Wrap one leaf of the plant with aluminum foil.
3. After a few days, unwrap the leaf. What has happened to the leaf? What color is it?

Observations: The plant leaf is no longer green.

Conclusions: A plant leaf will lose its green color without sunlight. Plants need sunlight to make food. When they do not get sunlight, their food factory shuts down, and the plants die. (Maybe you can still revive the leaf by giving it sunlight.)

Water, Please!

Plants need water to make and move nutrients around. How much water a plant needs depends on its size, its type, and its surrounding temperature. Too much or too little water can cause the plant to die. When the soil is slightly dry, it is time to water the plant.

Did you know that plants can drink fog? When it is foggy, tiny water drops float around in the air. Soil and plants can soak up the drops.

Lunch Menu

Except for the Venus flytrap, which catches insects almost like an animal does, most plants don't have a mouth to catch food. The nutrients that a plant needs come from the soil and are dissolved in water. The roots absorb the nutrients and carry them to the plant parts.

Three important plant nutrients are nitrogen, phosphorous, and potassium. Nitrogen is used for leafy growth and gives the plant its green color. Phosphorous is used for fruit production and root development. Potassium helps in many ways, including photosynthesis and plant sturdiness.

Roots carry water and nutrients.

Orchids

Epiphytic Plants

Epiphytic plants grow on other living plants and do not gather nutrients from the soil. Tropical orchids, mosses, and air plants are epiphytes. They get their water from moisture in the air and minerals from the surface of the plant on which they are growing.

Brrrr! It's Cold!

Plants like their surroundings to be comfortable. Some plants prefer warmer climates and others cooler temperatures. If you know the natural habitat of a plant, you can help it grow by making it comfortable.

Time to Grow!

Only in *Jack and the Beanstalk* does a bean plant grow tall overnight. Other plants take time to grow. If you watch a plant, you can't see it grow from minute to minute. But you can see it grow from day to day. It takes time for plants to grow. Some plants grow faster than others. The information on a package of seeds will usually tell you how long it will take for the plant to flower or bear fruit.

Fast Growers

One of the fastest-growing plants in the world is bamboo. Bamboo is a woody grass that is common in Asia and other parts of the world. Some forms have been recorded to grow up to three or four feet a day. In China, a bamboo plant has been measured to have grown approximately 153 feet in one year.

I Need Some Space!

Plants need space to grow. The part of the plant above the ground is called the *shoot*. The shoot needs space so the leaves can absorb sunlight and make food. Underneath the ground, the roots need space to expand and collect nutrients and water. If roots are crowded, the plant cannot grow well.

Mimosa

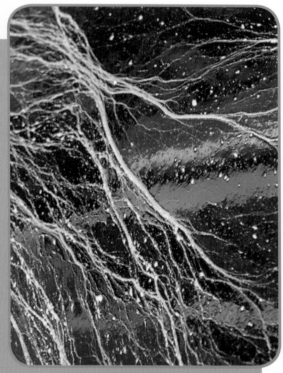
Roots need space to grow.

Shy Plants

Did you know that some plants are a little shy and sensitive, just like some people? One such plant is the mimosa plant. When you touch it, its leaves shy away and fold up. It takes about half an hour for the leaves to slowly unfold again. During hot weather, the leaves also fold up to protect the plant from burning.

PARTS OF A PLANT

Just like your body is made of many special parts with unique functions, plants also are made of different parts. Each part has an important job. Most plants have these key parts—roots, stems, flowers, fruits, seeds, and leaves.

Roots

Roots are usually under the ground to anchor the plant in the soil. They have tiny hairs that allow the plant to absorb water and nutrients from the soil. The roots serve as part of the plant's transportation system, carrying the water and minerals to the stem and leaves. Roots often store nutrients for later use.

Plants such as carrots and beets have a taproot system with one thick root and a few hairy branches. Plants such as grasses and wheat have a fibrous root system with a cluster of fine roots.

Stem

The stem is the main support of the plant and grows above the ground. It allows the leaves to gather the sunlight that they need to produce food. The stem also carries the water and nutrients that the roots absorb to the leaves. The leaves then move the food they produce to other parts of the plant. The xylem (ZEYE luhm) cells in the plant move water. The phloem (FLOH uhm) cells move food. Just like the roots, the stem may also store nutrients for later use.

Flowers

A plant's flowers are often the only things noticed about a plant. You don't usually see bouquets of stems or roots! Petals are the bright, colorful parts of the flower. Their colors and sweet aroma help attract bees, bats, moths, and butterflies, which help pollinate the flowers. Besides looking pretty and attracting insects, flowers have the important job of making seeds.

The **pistil** is the female part of the flower. It is in the center and has three parts—the stigma, style, and ovary. The stigma is the sticky bump at the top of the pistil. It is connected to a long tube called the *style*. The style connects the stigma to the ovary in the heart of the flower. Inside the ovary are units called **ovules** that contain eggs.

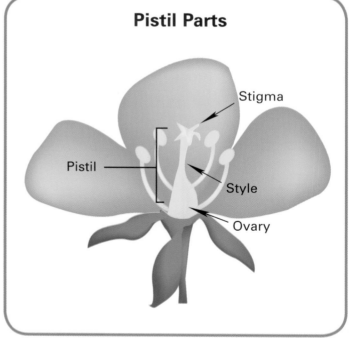

Pistil Parts

Stigma

Pistil

Style

Ovary

The **stamen** is the male, pollen-producing part of the plant. The stamen surrounds the pistil. The stamen has two parts—the anther and the filament. The filament supports the anther. The anther makes the pollen.

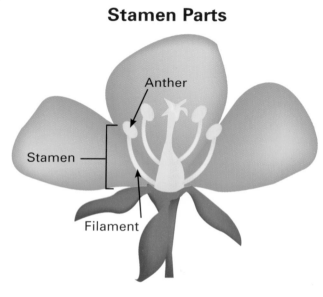

Stamen Parts

Anther

Stamen

Filament

The stamen of a flower

Fruit and Seeds

Once a plant has been pollinated, the ovary becomes the fruit. Inside the fruit, you find the seeds.

The fruit helps in the spreading of the seeds. For example, when a deer eats an apple, the apple seeds pass through the deer and are left elsewhere.

In some cases, the fruit helps protect the seed until it germinates. As an example, the shell of an acorn, which is part of the fruit, protects the seed within it from being easily eaten.

Every seed has what it takes to become a tiny plant with leaves, a stem, and roots. The parts are just waiting to germinate and grow. A seed coat protects the seed from outside forces until it is time for the embryo, or baby plant, to awaken and grow. This awakening is called *germination*.

A **cotyledon**, or seed leaf, is found inside the seed. Some plants have one cotyledon. They are called *monocots*. Corn is an example of a monocot. When plant seeds contain two cotyledons, they are called *dicots*. Beans are dicots. Cotyledons are the first leaves formed from a seed. These leaves help feed the new plant.

Leaves

If you look around, you will see that there are as many different kinds of leaves as there are kinds of plants. Simple leaves

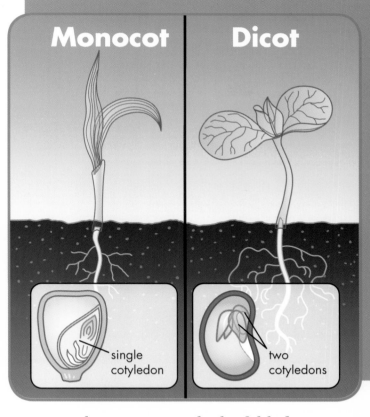

have one single leaf blade. A **petiole** connects it to the stem. Oak and maple leaves are simple leaves.

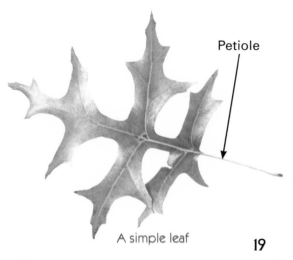

A simple leaf

19

Compound leaves have a leaf blade that is divided into separate leaflets. A petiole attaches them to the stem. Black walnut and honey locust have compound leaves.

Compound leaves of a black walnut

Parts of a Plant

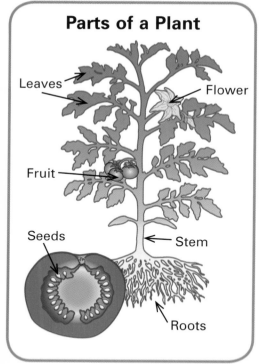

Leaves

Flower

Fruit

Seeds

Stem

Roots

Leaves catch sunlight and use it to make food. They have tiny openings to let water and air come in and go out. Veins in the leaves carry water and nutrients inside the leaf. Leaves have a shiny protective coating on the outside called a *cuticle.*

Plant Friends

Did you know that plants enjoy each other's company? What can you do with a plant whose leaves are droopy? Try placing it with other plants and it just might perk up.

A Plant's Food Factory

Did you know that plants make and use food? Just like you, plants need food to grow, to replace old cells, to dispose of waste, and to reproduce.

Photosynthesis

The process plants use to make food is called *photosynthesis*. In this process, plants combine carbon dioxide from the air with water that the plant absorbs from the soil. The sunlight's energy causes a chemical reaction that makes the food for the plants.

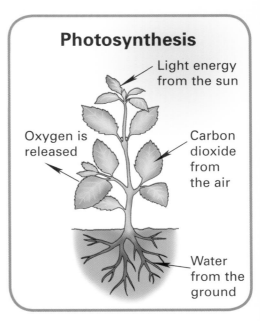

Photosynthesis

Light energy from the sun

Oxygen is released

Carbon dioxide from the air

Water from the ground

This food factory is inside the leaves in structures called *chloroplasts*. The chloroplasts contain **chlorophyll**, which is green-colored matter that absorbs energy from sunlight.

This absorbed energy joins with carbon dioxide and water to form oxygen and a sugar called *glucose*. The glucose feeds the plant, and the oxygen is released into the air.

> **Photosynthesis**
>
> **water + carbon dioxide + sunlight = sugar and oxygen**

Mushrooms

Are mushrooms plants? No, mushrooms are fungi. Fungi were once classified as plants, but now they are in their own category. They have no roots, stems, or leaves. They have many threads under the ground that bring water and food to the rest of the mushroom. The part above the ground makes spores that will germinate and become new mushrooms.

LIFE CYCLES OF PLANTS

A plant's life cycle is measured by how long the plant lives or how long it takes to grow, have flowers, and make seeds for the next cycle. That length of time varies for each species. Plants can be **annuals, biennials,** or **perennials**.

Annual Life Cycle

A cucumber is an annual plant.

The life cycle of an annual plant is one growing season. The seeds sprout, grow, flower, make more seeds, and die in one growing season. Cucumbers, pumpkins, petunias, peas, tomatoes, and corn are annual plants. The seeds need to be planted again every growing season.

Biennial Life Cycle

Biennial plants need two growing seasons to complete their life cycle. These plants grow during one season and then rest over the winter. They don't die at the end of the first season like an annual. During the second season, biennial plants grow flowers, make seeds, and then die. Parsley and carrots are biennial plants.

Perennial Life Cycle

Perennial plants live for more than two years. They grow, flower, and make seeds for many growing seasons in a row without having to be planted every season. Purple coneflowers and bleeding hearts are perennials. Other perennials, such as trees that change with the seasons, live for many years.

Parsley plant

Purple coneflower plants

PLANT POWER

What are you wearing?
What did you eat for dinner?
What is your house made of?
What do you inhale when you breathe?
What is this book made of?
The answers to all these questions involve plants.

Clothing

People use plants to make clothing. Clothing can be made of cotton, flax, or hemp. If you look at the tag on your shirt, you might see "100% Cotton." Sometimes the shirt is partly cotton and partly other fibers. You are wearing a plant.

Harvesting cotton in Mississippi

Food

Plants are the key source of all foods. How about your dinner? If you ate fried chicken with mashed potatoes, corn, a roll, and a glass of milk, most of your food can be tracked back to plants. Although a chicken is not a plant, it ate plants to survive. Potatoes and corn grew in a vegetable garden. The roll was made with flour that came from wheat. The milk came from a cow that ate grass to produce the milk.

Food chains start with plants.

All the food we eat in one way or another is connected to plants. A food chain starts with plants. Each link in a food chain tells who eats whom. People eat chickens that eat grass and seeds. There are three links in that food chain.

Shelter

Is your house or apartment made of wood? Parts of it, at least, are probably made with lumber. The wood was once a tree. Your school is also probably made of some wood.

Air

When you inhale, you breathe in oxygen. Plants are responsible for much of the oxygen in the air that you need to live.

Medicine

Many medicines have their origin in plants. Aspirin, herbal remedies, and some antibiotics come from plants.

Friedrich Bayer

Who Invented Aspirin?

Aspirin comes from plants. In 400 BC, the Greek physician Hippocrates discovered that the leaves and bark of the willow tree got rid of fever and pain. The ancient Romans also used willow bark to fight fevers. The bark and leaves of the willow tree are rich in a material called *salicin*. The use of this substance helped in the invention of aspirin.

Several inventors researched the effects of willow bark and leaves to come up with the origin of aspirin. In 1897, a German chemist, Felix Hoffman, with Friedrich Bayer and Company, researched a treatment for his father's pain. He found that acetylsalicylic acid, the chemical name for aspirin, worked in the same way as salicin, the ingredient found in willow bark and leaves. The chemist further developed the product and eventually introduced aspirin.

In 1899, the Bayer Company provided aspirin to physicians to give to their patients. It became the number-one drug. In 1952, inventors introduced children's chewable aspirin.

Books and Paper

Without plants, there would be no books or paper. Newspapers, magazines, and comic books are all made of paper. Paper comes from trees, which are plants.

From the clothing that you wear to the food that you eat to the books that you read, your world depends on plants.

Scientist of Significance

Jane Colden (1724–1766)

Jane Colden was America's first woman **botanist**. She published a book called *Botanic Manuscript*. It was one of the first books written about the characteristics of American plant life. She described the flora of her region—the plants, where they grew, and their names. She also included leaf prints and drawings of the many species of plants. Jane and her father, Cadwallader Colden, who was also a botanist, sent Jane's work to Carolus Linnaeus, a Swedish scientist. In 1753, Linnaeus invented a system for classifying plants and animals. Colden studied this system.

Internet Connections and Related Reading for

How Plants Grow

http://www.urbanext.uiuc.edu/gpe/gpe.html
Journey into the world of plants and solve mysteries with Bud, Sprout, and Detective LePlant. The Great Plant Escape Web site comes from the University of Illinois Extension.

http://www.kidport.com/RefLib/Science/HowPlantsGrow/HowPlantsGrow.htm
Read more about how plants grow.

http://library.thinkquest.org/3715/root2.html
Click on this page to learn more about plants and their function in the environment.

http://biology.clc.uc.edu/courses/bio104/photosyn.htm
Would you like to read more about photosynthesis? Visit this Web site for more information.

Experiments with Plants by Salvatore Tocci. Hands-on experiments with plants. Children's Press, 2001. ISBN 0-5162-7351-5 (PB) 0-6135-4211-8 (HB) [RL 4.2 IL 3–5] (6871601 PB 6871606 HB)

From Seed to Plant by Gail Gibbons. Explores the relationship between seeds and the plants they produce. Holiday House, 1991. ISBN 0-8234-0872-8 [RL 2.9 IL K–3] (5843406 HB)

How a Seed Grows by Helene J. Jordan. Explains how a seed grows into a plant. HarperCollins, 1992. ISBN 0-0644-5107-0 [RL 2 IL K–4] (8131401 PB)

How Plants Grow by Malcolm Penny. Describes how plants grow. Benchmark Books, 1997. ISBN 0-0602-0104-5 [RL 4.6 IL 3–7] (5896306 HB)

Plant Growth by Louise and Richard Spilsbury. Learn more about the growth of plants. Heinemann, 2003. ISBN 1-4034-0502-6 [RL 3 IL 3–5] (3453201 PB)

• RL = Reading Level
• IL = Interest Level
Perfection Learning's catalog numbers are included for your ordering convenience. PB indicates paperback. HB indicates hardback.

GLOSSARY

airborne (AIR born) carried by or through the air

annual
(AN nyou wuhl) plant that flowers, produces seed, and dies in one growing season

biennial
(bi EN nee uhl) plant that lives for two years and produces flowers and fruit in the second year

botanist
(BAHT nist) person who studies plants

chlorophyll
(KLOR uh fil) green-colored matter that absorbs light energy for photosynthesis

chloroplast
(KLOR uh plast) sac that contains chlorophyll and is the place where photosynthesis occurs within plant cells

conifer (KAHN uh fur) cone-producing trees and shrubs

cotyledon
(kah tuh LEE duhn) seed leaf of a plant used to supply nutrients for the developing seedling

cuticle
(KYOU tik uhl) shiny coating that protects the outside of leaves

epiphytic
(ep uh FIT tik) living on the surface of plants

habitat
(HAB uh tat) home or place where organisms live

nutrient
(NEW tree uhnt) food; substance consumed for energy or to help maintain the organism

ovule
(AHV youl) the female plant part that develops into seeds

perennial
(puh REN nee uhl) plant that lasts for more than two growing seasons, either dying back after each season or growing continuously

petiole
(PET tee ohl) joins the leaf to the main stem

photosynthesis
(foh toh SIN thuh suhs) the process by which a plant makes its food using energy from the sun, carbon dioxide from the air, and water from the soil

pistil
(PIS tuhl) female part of the flower that consists of the stigma, style, and ovary

pollination
(pah luh NAY shuhn) process of placing pollen on the stigma

stamen
(STAY muhn) the male part of the flower which consists of the anther and filament

INDEX

ISBN: 981-4068-72-1
Cambodia and Angkor, A travel sketchbook.
Damien Chavanat ◆ Elsie ◆ Justin Creedy Smith
© Éditions du Seuil, 27, rue Jacob, 75006 Paris, France 2003 for the French version
www.seuil.com
© Justin Creedy Smith for the photographs.
© Elsie and Damien Chavanat for the text and illustrations.

This edition is published by
Archipelago Press,
an imprint of
Editions Didier Millet
121, Telok Ayer Street, # 03-01
Singapore 068590
www.edmbooks.com
In association with Krousar Thmey, Phnom Penh, Cambodia.

CAMBODIA & ANGKOR

LES 3 MOUSTIQUAIRES

We would like to thank their Majesties, the King and the Queen of Cambodia.

In memory of Alain and Jean-Marie.

A big thank you to Benito, without whom this project would not have happened.
He welcomed us to Cambodia and supported us, materially and morally,
throughout the making of this book.

We would like to thank, in particular, Béatrice Le Guay and Zahia Hafs
for their precious help and enthusiasm during the long hours spent elaborating
the text and the layout.

Our thanks to Marie-Claude and Didier Millet, Valérie Millet and Heimata Champs,
at Les Editions du Pacifique for their collaboration.

Our thanks to Lisa Barnett for her attentive proofreading.

Our thanks to Jacques Binsztok, Claude Hénard and Sabine Louali
at Les Editions du Seuil

Our thanks to Michel Renaud and Éric Gauthey,
founders of the "Biennale du carnet de voyage", Clermont-Ferrand, France.

Our thanks to Arnaud Lebonnois and to Lonely Planet.

Our thanks to Anne Chapoutot, Marie-Jo and Bernard Chavanat, Hélène, Véronique,
Louis and Odile Chavanat, Geneviève Contesso, Jane and Peter Creedy Smith,
Rafika Degachi, Pierre Delbon, Kerya Eng Sun, Marcel Georges, Isabelle Jarry,
Geneviève Marot, Véronique and Hans Schwimann, the Truong family
and Aleth Vignon for their help.

Our thanks to Stéphanie, Sandra and Pierre-Marie, volunteers at Krousar Thmey.

Our thanks to Pascale Baret and Gilles Ringwald of Thaï Airways, Sylvain Brosseau
of Kodak for the Portra films, Patricia Gassmann, François George and Bou Ming
Ang of Picto, Isabelle Jordan-Ghizzo, Nathalie Tollu and Nello Zoppé.

A big thank you to all those who have supported us, far and wide,
since the publication of *Zanzibar, carnets de voyage*.

Justin dedicates this book to Florence, Clara and Eliza.

Elsie Herberstein would like to thank "le Centre National du Livre" for the
creative writing grant they awarded her.

To support **Krousar Thmey**

CAMBODIA 4, rue 257, Avenue Kampuchea Krom, Phnom Penh ◆ **FRANCE** 10, rue Dussoubs, 75002 Paris ◆ **SWITZERLAND** c/o CRAM, 63, rue de Lausanne, 1202 Genève

www.krousar-thmey.org

CAMBODIA & ANGKOR

Damien Chavanat ◆ Elsie ◆ Justin Creedy Smith
Translated by Lisa Davidson

Archipelago Press

A VISIT TO
Cambodia
IS A MUST

A bord de nos Services CARAVELLE vous rencontrerez à la fois le confort d'un voyage rapide en Jet et tout le charme d'un accueil fidèle à l'une des plus anciennes civilisations.

INTRODUCTION

Damien slips his childhood book into his bags.

Trappes, outside Paris 1969

Damien is eight years old. At school, his best friends are Patrick and Roland. Their father Marcel is a disabled soldier. Drafted as a young man to serve in the Indochina War, he lost a leg and an arm after stepping on a land mine in Vietnam. Yet he often leaves home to travel the world. Recently he has started taking his elder son with him, with the aim of producing short illustrated books. These tell the story of his son and a child from the country they visit. This year, they have just returned from Cambodia. The result is the publication of two books, Roland in Cambodia and Roland and the Golden Statuette, which Damien still has. After school, he often goes to play with his friends. The apartment is filled with all sorts of souvenirs that Marcel has brought back from his trips abroad. His favourite place is the spot housing the photographs of the Angkor temples and a few statuettes, copies of Khmer art masterpieces. For Damien, Angkor became a distant and magical Eden, a place he dreamed of visiting one day.

Serville, Ile de France, 1992

It's Pentecost. The table is laid outside under the old roses. Béatrice and Denys left Paris three years ago to live in a village in the Beauce region. Béatrice has been a close friend ever since we travelled together to the Tassili du Hoggar in the Sahara. She has invited me to meet an unusual friend, Benito. I don't know much about him, except that he lives in Thailand and Cambodia, and that he has just created his own non-governmental organisation (NGO) to help refugee Cambodian children. In 1990, he was working as an accountant in Bangkok for the Accor Asie hotel group, when he spent a weekend at the Site II camp, set up by the United Nation (U.N.) for Cambodian refugees on the Thai border; some 215,000 people were crowded into an area of 7.6 square kilometres. He returned to Bangkok, overwhelmed. He decided to take a sabbatical year to work for a small French NGO teaching accountancy. At the same time, he opened his first protection centre inside the Site II camp. It took care of 35 abandoned children and supported 35 other members from the same families. Krousar Thmey, "new family" in Khmer, was born. Benoît became known as "Benito", without realising that this nickname would replace his real name. At the same time, a peace agreement was signed among the various political factions, ending twenty-one years of civil war. The refugees could finally think about returning to Khmer soil. Leaving the cramped quarters of an enclosure surrounded by barbed wire the many children born in the camps would soon arrive in a country

they had never before seen. Benito mounted a large exhibition about Khmer heritage and about the reality of Cambodian life. It was a huge success: 35,000 children from families representing every different political faction discovered their past. After one year Benito had to make a decision: return to work for Accor or undertake the creation of a children's foundation. He planned to organise small projects, which would be more efficient and easier to manage, and to hire only foreign volunteers to help with the administrative work. His priority was to train Cambodians to take care of their own children. After eight months of obstacles and interference, he managed to obtain the necessary governmental authorisations to repatriate the children under his care. On November, 2nd 1992 the first Krousar Thmey children arrived at Siem Reap, two kilometres from the Angkor temples; and on February, 3rd 1993 those left at Site II were placed at Takmau, south of Phnom Penh. Before the end of the year, a third child protection centre had opened in Sisophon, with the support of UNICEF.

Béatrice's garden, where I first met Benito.

The protective butterfly, logo of Krousar Thmey, khmer for "new family".

 គ្រួសារថ្មី

Benoît Duchâteau Arminjon, known as "Benito", is the founder of Krousar Thmey, now the most important child care NGO in Cambodia.

As he does every summer, Benito returned to Europe to meet with his principal sponsors and to find new support. He shared his concerns with us. The United Nations had arrived in Cambodia to help organise the elections to be held in May 1993, sending 120,000 personnel to the country. Rents in Phnom Penh had rocketed, rising from 300 to 3,000 dollars a month. Krousar Thmey did not have the money to rent anything at all, and Benito was selling his Parisian apartment, in the Ménilmontant district, to purchase a house with a terrace in the west of Phnom Penh. This is where he intended to set up the headquarters of his NGO, along with a restaurant, "La Casa", which he hoped would generate additional funds for Krousar Thmey.

I didn't see Benito again—until last year. In the meantime, Béatrice had maintained an intense correspondence with him and kept me informed of his progress. His restaurant had become one of the best in the capital. The first centres were operating well and he had turned his attention to other urgent issues. The streets of Phnom Penh were filled with homeless children, adolescents who had run away, escaping the countryside for the city streets. Benito opened a temporary shelter in 1993. He then launched a crusade to help disabled children, especially the deaf and blind. It all started with Wanna, an 11-year-old blind boy abandoned in a hospital at the Site II camp. Krousar Thmey took him in at one of the centres, but he had no access to any education. No program for the blind had ever been developed in Cambodia. Benito had no special knowledge in this area, but with the help of Madame Neang Phalla, a Cambodian who agreed to leave her job with the United Nations (and a 50 percent cut in wages), he founded the first school for blind children in 1994. In addition to the purchase of land and construction costs, schoolbooks needed to be translated into Braille and competent teachers to be trained. He was running out of money but, fortunately, a Thai foundation and King Sihanouk came to his rescue. In 1997, two schools for the

11

Site II camp, on the Thai border.

After 21 years of war the refugees, and many children born in the camps, can return to Cambodia at last.
Krousar Thmey opens its first two centres, in Siem Reap and Phnom Penh.

deaf were opened. There are now more than a dozen throughout the country. It was a wonderful success, but it is still a constant struggle. In Poipet, on the Thai border, a city of smugglers and trafficking, a handful of soldiers and local mafia are getting rich through the systematic exploitation of the very poor. It is particularly important that Krousar Thmey should be present there. A shelter for single mothers and their children, another for the homeless and a school have all been built. One day, the director of the school called Benito, panic-stricken. Soldiers had confiscated half of their land to build casinos. Benito counterattacked in court. He received a number of death threats and, despite armed guards with Kalachnikovs at his home, he went through a very difficult period. After several months he considered giving up, as it seemed impossible to solve the problem and he was in physical danger. Instead he pulled himself together and launched new projects.

Paris, 1993

Cambodia is finally liberated. After meeting with several young journalists working in the area, Damien participated in the creation of a French weekly published in Phnom Penh, entitled *Le Mékong*. He then planned to visit the capital and put together the outlines for a travel notebook. Nothing came of the project, being premature.

Zanzibar, 1998

This was our second trip to this paradise island off the coast of Tanzania. Damien and I had fallen in love with it last summer after travelling through Africa. This time we took along Justin, our English photographer friend, with the idea of creating a "three-way" travel notebook. We had wanted to work together for a long time, to combine our individual viewpoints and techniques into a single work: Damien with his illustrations and graphic design; Justin, his photographic portraits; and myself, alternating sketches and narrative. Our little team, nicknamed

"Les Trois Moustiquaires", literally "The Three Mosquito Nets" in French, and was born in the lively streets of Stone Town. Our first book, *Zanzibar, carnets de voyage*, was published two years later.

During book-signing sessions, many people asked about our next destination. At the time it was still a secret, but we had already discussed it amongst ourselves: Cambodia was the obvious choice.

Paris, Montparnasse station, July 2001

Montparnasse station: I'm scanning the crowd on the platform, trying to catch sight of Benito. After ten years, I'm not sure I'll recognise him. Béatrice jumped at the chance of a rare and short Parisian trip to invite us, once again, to one of her outdoor luncheons. In the end, Benito spots me, tapping me on the shoulder. He hasn't changed. His eyes are as bright and cheeky as ever. It seems to me that he is even better looking now that he's older. And he's still only thirty five!

I learn with amazement that he has partially retired, delegating all his operational duties to a Cambodian director, Thary. Now a volunteer, he continues to devote 30 percent of his time to fund-raising and planning a global strategy for Krousar Thmey. For a living, he teaches classes at the university, performs audits and has just opened a hotel in Siem Reap—Borann, l'Auberge des Temples. We celebrate meeting up again and the success of Krousar Thmey, which in ten years has become the leading Cambodian foundation for underprivileged children. It runs some thirty projects, schools and cultural centres. Benito looks through *Zanzibar* carefully and says, enthusiastically: "So now, all you have to do is work on another one about Cambodia!" Our trip home is filled with excited discussion about the plan and I watch, without believing it, a dream transform into reality. I still remember Damien's expression when I got home and said: "In three months time, we're off to Phnom Penh".

LES 3 MOUSTIQUAIRES

Justin, the photographer, Elsie and Damien, the artists, go to Zanzibar in 1998, to create their first book together.

13

FIRST VOYAGE
PHNOM PENH

SALLE D'ATTENTE ICI
PLEASE WAIT HERE

CUSTOMS DEPARTMENT CAMBODIA

PASSENGER'S DECLARATION

'I CERTIFY THAT ALL STATEMENTS ON THIS DECLARATION ARE TRUE, COMPLETE AND CORRECT.'

We've only just got off the plane and have already created confusion among the customs officers, by inadvertently swapping passports and visas!

25th November 2001, Pochentong Airport

It's 9:30am, after a sleepless fifteen-hour-long night flight, a six-hour time difference and a stopover in Bangkok. The airport is brand-spankingly new. An official military delegation stands at attention on the runway, awaiting the arrival of a distinguished Vietnamese visitor—an event confirmed by the flags flying on the main building. We feel dishevelled and somewhat disoriented, having never set foot in Asia before. We therefore forget the protocol of presenting ourselves individually at the passport control and not in twos. Annoyed, the policeman waves Damien off to the next counter, and asks me, without explanation, to fill out the immigration form a second time. I protest, and open my passport to show that I have already filled it out, when I realise it's not my passport. The policeman immediately understands what's

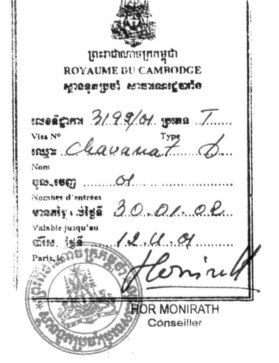

ROYAUME DU CAMBODGE

Visa N°   Type

Nom

Nombre d'entrées

Valable jusqu'au

Paris, le

HOR MONIRATH
Conseiller

14

Phnom Penh traffic: two-wheeled vehicles all over the place, narrowly avoiding each other. The drivers are, no doubt, inured to this and have developed a kind of extra sensory perception that alerts them to obstacles and dangers.

M-150

M-150

เส้น 150

เมล็ดแตงโม
M16

Avenue "Kampuchea Krom" swarming, dusty and noisy. To help us find our way, we've chosen a building that looks like a huge birthday cake!

sides or holding a package, they somehow manage to keep their balance, despite the many potholes and the constant need to brake sharply. Others sway dangerously under the pyramid of objects they're transporting. This chaotic crowd slaloms its way among the cars, horns blasting, and protected from the dust by a light cotton mask or a krama plastered against their faces, a bunch of urban bandits. The city has a provincial look to it, although new buildings are springing up everywhere. Damien is sitting in the back, silent. I can sense his excitement at being surrounded by all these bikes and motorcycles. There's so much to see and so much happening that I am, like him, overwhelmed by the newness of it all. I try to capture and to absorb all the sights, sounds and smells that I can. Nothing can compare to this feeling of the "first time".

La Casa

"La Casa", halfway between the airport and the city centre along Kampuchea Krom Avenue, is the headquarters of Krousar Thmey, consisting of two white houses with large green shutters and flat terraced rooftops.

There's no one around, apart from the two guards who open the entrance gate and help unload our bags. The offices are closed on Sunday, and the other volunteers are out of town and expected to return during the evening, or the next day. Before going back to bed, Florent makes us some coffee and gives us a few good tips for the day: he recommends walking along the river banks, near the Royal Palace, the Sisowath Quay lined with gardens, restaurants and cafés, and visiting the National Museum.

Public transportation is non-existent. To get around, everyone uses motodops, scooters that carry one, two and even three passengers. There are also rickshaws, but these are slower. The prices, in dollars or riels (one dollar = 3,900 riels) should be negotiated before you start, to avoid confrontation on arrival. Apparently it's best to steer clear of an angry Cambodian.

happened and turns toward his colleague, who has just let Damien go through, after stamping and stapling "his" form onto "my" passport. In a heated exchange the former policeman reprimands the latter, but things end with a burst of laughter and a sigh of relief as we pass through customs.

At the exit we look around for a sign marked Krousar Thmey, but we don't see anything. A 4x4 soon brakes to a halt in front of us. A young man in jeans and a tee shirt, wearing a krama[1] tied into a turban, jumps out and greets us. Florent has been a volunteer in Phnom Penh[2] for a year and a half and is in charge of public relations and communication for the NGO. It is six kilometres from Pochentong Airport to the headquarters of Krousar Thmey. The traffic, along the wide avenues, is horrendous, with hundreds of two-wheeled vehicles carrying from two up to five passengers! Sitting bolt upright, arms dangling at their

On the corner of
Kampuchea Krom
and 257 avenues,
"la Casa" is home to
the Krousar Thmey
offices and also provides
accommodation for foreign
voluntary workers and
passing visitors.

PHNOM PENH -

17

La Croisette

The official portraits of King Norodom and Queen Monineath.

Siesta time:
Strollers converse in small groups, sitting on the lawn. Others sleep, lying on the balustrade or under a tree. The welcome shade of the pagoda, opposite the Royal Palace, attracts visitors and the faithful. Many of them burn incense sticks or leave offerings of lotus flowers and fruit.

Coming back from the market:
brake suddenly and it's
Runny omelette for lunch.

I come upon some bird-sellers,
who want me to buy a bird
to set it free. This is also
a way of venerating Bouddha.
What the tourists don't
know is that the bird
flies back, and is
returned to its
cage to be
sold again.

19

gangs of children,
stationed along the riverside,
look out for strollers, hoping
to polish their shoes or
beg a few riels.

La croisette

With two of us on the back our motodop winds through the traffic on Kampuchea Krom Avenue, which runs in a straight line to the city centre. We cross other major boulevards—the Mao Tse Tung, the Sivutha, the Monivong—before reaching a strange star-shaped structure topped with a dark yellow dome, an Art Deco gem. This is Psar Thmei[3], the central market and one of the largest in Phnom Penh, where anything can be found.

The motodop drops us off on Sisowath Quay, opposite the Royal Palace, where the two rivers, the Tonle Sap and the Mekong, flow together. Viewed from the promenade, they appear to be very distinct. On one side is the clear blue water of the Tonle Sap and on the other, the enormous muddy flow of the mighty Mekong. Once a year, however, a unique phenomenon occurs: during the rainy season, from May to October—which is also when the Himalayan snows melt—the Mekong rises so fast and powerfully that it doubles-back into the Tonle Sap. The direction of its flow is reversed for over one hundred kilometres, the waters surging upstream as far as the lake, which floods as a result.

We are soon surrounded by a group of children, including a small girl who is pulling a legless child on a board; he is not a mine victim, but one of the many children disabled at birth or from childhood diseases. They beg for a few riels and offer to polish our shoes. Damien is persuaded, handing over his old docksiders, grabbed at by the boy quickest off the mark. The others watch as we draw. We walk back toward the central market. I notice a group of children approaching. They are in a sorry state: dirty, ragged and staring blankly. Two of them, the youngest—they're hardly four or five years old—are holding pale-coloured plastic bags from which they repeatedly take sniffs. This is my first contact with the glue-sniffing street children.

For the first few kilometres we hang on tight to the driver, then we get over our fear and settle back to enjoy the ride.

21

On the look out for some where to get a bite to eat, we find a
little open-air market where women sell ready-made
dishes under patchwork parasols. Everything looks
mouthwatering: I choose marinated fish and frogs' legs,
with rice and boiled cabbage. I sit on one of the
multi-coloured plastic stools that are inevitable features
of pavements, restaurants and markets all over Southeast Asia.

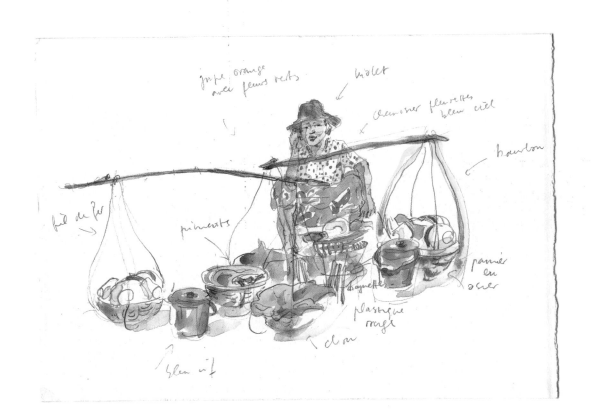

Two women, carrying baskets on each end
of a pole, dodge in and out of the
traffic to cross the street. The vibration
of the bamboo on their shoulders
puts a spring in their step.
They squat down on the pavement
to unpack their ustensils:
earthenware bowls, plastic
buckets, chopsticks, spoons
and sieves, and their
ingredients: cabbages, peppers,
chillis, onions, citronella
and chicken stock.

The "Psar Thmei"
OR
Central Market.

Built by the French in the 1930s
in pure Art Déco Style, it is one of the biggest
markets in Phnom Penh and the landmark
that helps us to find our way.

Around the market, there are shops, whose windows can be seen from afar, all with fairy lights on. They don't actually sell Christmas decorations, but jewellery. Cambodians prefer to invest in gold, being more stable than currency.

25

Motodops carry two, three, four and even five passengers. Families arrange themselves with one child on the handlebars, another sandwiched between the parents, and a baby nestled between the mother's breasts.

Monday, 26th November
Inauguration of the Lake Tonle Sap exhibition at the Wat Lang Ka pagoda[4]

Pascal and Cécile are the most recent volunteers with Krousar Thmey. Pascal works in forestry and Cécile is a teacher. They decided to spend a year in Cambodia and, after a period of training and acclimatisation, they are preparing to leave Phnom Penh for several months touring around the lake. Their aim is to present a travelling exhibition about the Lake Tonle Sap to as many schools and people as possible. We leave at 8:am and head towards the Independence Monument. The capital is celebrating the first visit by the Vietnamese president in several years. A planned trip the previous year was cancelled after a bomb blew up a government building in Phnom Penh, killing four people and injuring several others. This is a first, therefore, and very symbolic, as relations between Cambodia and Vietnam are anything but simple. Although Vietnam liberated Cambodia from the Khmer Rouge, the Vietnamese

are the hereditary enemies of Cambodians—who are mistrustful and deeply resent the ten-year occupation.

The schoolchildren have arrived already in the courtyard. Little girls in blue and white uniforms play hopscotch under a banyan tree, the sacred tree of the pagodas. The exhibition has been set up in an outbuilding near the pagoda and Madame Kosal, who assists Thary, Krousar Thmey's director, is busy at a table carefully arranging refreshments for the visitors.

The children sit on the ground, girls on one side, boys on the other, waiting their turn to visit the exhibition. I take advantage of their temporary stillness to carefully observe them, trying to understand their bone structure, features and facial expressions. Since arriving I've had difficulty capturing an Asian feel to my drawings; I am still under the influence of my many previous trips to Africa.

Benito finally arrives with a man in his sixties, who has an air of Captain Haddock about him. His flowery voice is pitched above everyone else's and he quickly dominates,

In the courtyard, under a banyan tree, classes of schoolchildren in uniform wait their turn to visit the Tonle Sap exhibition.

Philippe Magnier,
a retired geological engineer,
is president of Krousar
Thmey in France.

Lundi 26 novembre

Phnom Penh
Le monument de l'indépendance

Les milliers de petits drapeaux aux couleurs des deux pays
honorent la visite du premier ministre cambodgien.
Les banderoles bleues indiquent l'entrée de l'exposition de Krousar Thmey.

29

In the inner
courtyard, monks
worship the statue
of the "leper king",
which has been kept
under glass since
being moved
from its original
throne at
Angkor Thom.

then monopolises, the conversation. Philippe Magnier has been the tireless and efficient president of Krousar Thmey since 1992. Now retired, he used to work as a geological engineer for Total, living and specialising in Southeast Asia for most of his career. He is a talented fund-raiser and runs the Paris office. Once or twice a year he pays his own way to Cambodia to check on the operations of the Krousar Thmey centres scattered around the country.

Damien and Benito are in the courtyard of the pagoda with two young boys, who are apprentice shoemakers. Damien is not sure about giving them his worn-out and partially torn shoes. He had planned to throw them away and buy others at the market. Benito reassures him: "Give them your shoes, you'll see, they'll fix them in no time." The two boys each readily grab a shoe and share the job: one prepares the shoe by removing the old stitching and kneading it to make it more supple, while the other unwinds the new thread. I follow every movement, observing the dexterity and rapidity with which he stretches the thread between his toes, knotting it, then threading it through the punched leather, sewing it back together with perfect precision. These two, like the shoeshine boys we

PHNOM PENH - NATIONAL MUSEUM - NOV. 2001

BENITO MÉDITE...

saw yesterday and like most of the small street enterprises and vendors are, in fact, Vietnamese. Despite the suspicion they arouse and rejection they receive, there are still many Vietnamese in Cambodia and, combined with the Chinese, they form a powerful and essential business community. Clear-minded and hard-working, they flourish and integrate easily into the society.

National Museum

After lunch, we set off to visit the National Museum, which—along with the Guimet Museum in Paris—houses the largest collection of Khmer art in the world. It's a lovely red brick building, constructed in a traditional architectural style by George Groslier[5] around 1920. The museum is surrounded by gardens, which back onto the School of Fine Arts.

At first, I am not aware of the exceptional beauty and rarity of each object. Rather, I am overcome by the atmosphere; that of a sleepy provincial museum, bathed in a dusky half-light, rays of sunshine transforming the dusty air into a fine golden mist. In an ancient ritual gesture, both of devotion and of preservation, women sweep every nook and cranny endlessly—yet, watching the brooms swish to and fro, I wonder about the effectiveness of all this as the dust swirls up, is caught in the sunlight and settles elsewhere. Others, guards and worshippers, slip ahead of the tourists. They are holding bouquets of dried jasmine in their slender hands, which they will place for you on the altar of one of the many divinities, in exchange for a few coins. Totally absorbed by the works, I hadn't noticed a persistent, and unusual, background noise: a regular squeaking, punctuated by sudden screeches. It sounds like a cicada, but one I've never heard before— simply because it's made by bats! Thousands of these creatures live in the roof of the museum and their droppings are so corrosive that they have eroded the ceilings and damaged the artwork on display. Australia came to the rescue of the museum—and the bats, threatened with extermination—by financing the construction of a stronger roof. Thanks to this work, visitors can still watch a cloud of black wings taking off from the rooftops at sunset.

Friends

Not far from the museum, farther down the road next door to the Café des Beaux-Arts, is the headquarters of "Friends", a humanitarian organisation working to help street children. Sébastien Marot, a 38-year-old Frenchman, is one of the founders and directors. His sister, an illustrator in Paris, gave us a package and letter for him. Benito knows him, as they work in the same domain and support each other. The NGOs (non-governmental organisations)—of which there are more than 250 in Cambodia—are not always on the best of terms. Each defends its own cause and its own interests. The constant search for funds, and everything that that involves, creates friction between the different organisations.

The centre looks like a school playground, facing the street. There's a lot going on; it's filled with children and adolescents, all under the watchful eyes of young Western and Cambodian volunteers, wearing "Friends" tee shirts. It's time for the school bus to take the youngsters home. Small trucks nicknamed "salad shakers" (after the grill protecting the rear of the van) take the children back to the slums where they live with their families or in groups. Access to the centre is free. Children can come and go as they please, there is neither a requirement to attend, nor an imposed schedule.

We walk toward the offices on the first floor, and suddenly Sébastien dashes down the stairs: one of the squats, where "Friends" has rooms housing children, is reported to be on fire. He has to get there as fast as possible to check the damage and salvage whatever he can. Once again the fire is the talk of the town, more than

likely a voluntary "accident" caused by those people interested in regaining the land, which has increased greatly in value in the last few years.

Phnom Penh, by night

As we return to "La Casa", I notice strange lumpy black rectangles along the pavements on Kampuchea Krom Avenue, surrounded by bags of sand, that weren't there yesterday. Two men climb out of a hole in the road, carrying sacks that they dump on the ground, forming the rectangles, each one measuring about two metres by five metres. To prevent flooding during the rainy season, the city's sewage workers regularly dig up and bring all this

Night falls suddenly, at 6 pm, and the traffic gets heavier. Perhaps the little boy hanging onto the handlebars is dreaming of Father Christmas!

The child in the middle reminds me uncannily of my favourite painting by Egon Schiele.

refuse to the surface, where they leave it to dry for several days. Trucks then pick it up and take it outside the city.

It's 8pm and the nightlife is in full swing. "La Casa" is surrounded by video game arcades and pool halls. We are drawn to the flashy facades of certain hotels lining the wide avenues. All offer karaoke bars, which front as rooms for rent by the hour "with girls", and many are owned by influential people or military officers. Contrary to common belief, prostitution is not entirely due to Westerners visiting Cambodia on sex tours. In fact, they represent only a small percentage of the market. After dinner many Asian men visit these bars with their friends to hire prostitutes.

On the way back, we want to stop at "Heart of Darkness", a favourite with Phnom Penh's in-crowd, but the bar is closed. Two days before our arrival, the government voted in a law prohibiting bars from opening at night, officially in order to reduce crime and violence. This is the first time such a law has been strictly applied, and many people think it won't last for long—the owners will soon find a way to side-step it. Already, the bar opposite is open. It's one of those bars that cater to an exclusively Western male clientele. Under the vigilant eye of the "madame" in charge, young girls sidle up to their clients, encouraging them to drink and snuggling up provocatively. On the other side of the street, small children, wide-awake, observe closely the goings-on from a first-floor balcony. Their parents don't seem to mind.

Sihanoukville

Tuesday, 27th November
From Phnom Penh to Sihanoukville

We wake up early as we're leaving for Sihanoukville. It's 232 kilometres from Phnom Penh to the country's leading port via National Highway 4, the only negotiable road in Cambodia. The road leading out of Phnom Penh is colourful and lively. Through the window, I see a succession of gleaming pagodas, several under construction, and many gigantic schools, their grassy play areas dotted with small blue and white figures. There are children everywhere: 50 percent of the population is under the age of fifteen. This fact is even more striking in that we hardly see any old people. Very few survived the genocide, and even today, not many live past fifty. Several factories line the road. One appears to be new ; although constructed some time ago to produce noodles, it has never opened in fact. More than likely it was a foreign investor who pulled out at the last minute. Unfortunately, foreign investment is in freefall now, 50 percent lower in 2001 than in the previous year. Today the only major investments are in the tourist industry in Siem Reap and the textile factories around Phnom Penh.

Despite lower wages, the lack of infrastructure, widespread corruption and lower productivity than in neighbouring countries dissuade many companies from investing in Cambodia. Yet there is an urgent need to provide employment for the emerging generation flooding the job market. The educated and cultural elite was either decimated by the Khmer Rouge or is in exile. The country, lacking education and a humanist ideology, is more often than not ruled by the "dollar." Destabilised by years of civil war, and ruled by a government which cannot afford to pay its own civil servants a proper salary, corruption is rampant at all levels, bringing the economic development to a standstill. Salaries are so low that people do whatever they can to make a bit on the side. I was surprised at a swindle run by the police. They stop all the trucks and taxis at crossroads, skimming off a "tax" to augment their take-home pay. A friendly "handshake" actually conceals the transfer of a small banknote to the policeman. Everything is taxed and everything can be bought at a price: a driving license, a university degree, a professorship, a position as accountant, a custom officer's or civil servant's job.

We are now in the countryside: rice paddies stretch as far the eye can see, interspersed with hundreds of palm trees, their shaggy foliage perched atop flexible, spindly trunks. It's a good time to be here: the rainy season is over, as are the floods. The water is gradually starting to recede and nature is at her very best, the sun glistening on the water-soaked land. The rice harvest has just started and will continue until February.

On the Pich Nil pass.
"Grandma Mao's"
infamous place of
pilgrimage.

A man of little
multicoloured altars
lined up opposite
two humble pagodas.

Every car makes
a brief stop:
the driver dashes to
the pagoda, puts
his hands together
in a greeting to the
statue of Buddha,
slips a banknote
into the slot in the
urn, lights some
incense, then disappears
into the shrubbery
to relieve himself.
He then leaves, safe
in the knowledge
that he is protected
by "good spirits".

35

Rural houses are plain, simple and attractive, and are always of the same design: a wooden hut with railings, built on stilts, with a sloping tiled roof. The houses are raised not only to stock animals and against the risk of flooding, but also because this creates an area of shade—the only place to be during the hot weather. Bright-coloured, frilly curtains add a note of jollity. The essential hammock, a cliché of Cambodian life, is suspended between the stilts under the house, and there is often a daybed, a square, short-legged platform, on which the family sits cross-legged around a meal. Each house has a sort of garden where people could easily grow vegetables. Unfortunately, vegetable gardens are rare, and most of the fruit and vegetables eaten by Cambodians come from neighbouring countries. The roadside stalls in the villages we drive through sell juicy-looking pineapples hanging on strings. We stop to buy some. Once again, the vendors are either Chinese or Vietnamese and the pineapples come from Thailand. To keep me from total despair, Benito assures me that the bananas, at least, are grown locally.

The landscape is becoming hillier. We are halfway and are approaching the Elephant Mountains, Chuor Phnom Damrei, an extension of the Cardamom Mountains, which run along the Thai border. Where we cross the mountains the altitude is lower, and the slopes melt away into bluish rolling hills.

Kompong Som Bay

It's almost noon, and we're close to the sea. We're on the last leg, and as the road drops to the coast Kompong Som, also known as Sihanoukville, unfolds before us. In the 1950s, as part of major plans to develop his country, the king had the French build a large, modern, deep-water port. This was the ideal site for this ambitious project.

We leave the port and fishing village to our right, driving along the coast towards the city centre and the resort. Krousar Thmey has set up a project for street

children, teaching them how to sail and to fish, as motivation to leave the streets of Phnom Penh and take control of their own lives. We reach the headquarters, and meet those who work part-time for the project. Than and Monsieur Pech Bin are to join us for lunch. They have been in charge since 1995, when it was launched.

The initial idea was simple: a concrete project for problem children. The adolescents choose to come voluntarily on a three-month programme in Sihanoukville. Than and Monsieur Pech Bin, assisted by French specialist fishermen, try to train them. Krousar Thmey has three trawlers. They go to sea early in the morning. The rest of the day the children attend classes learning the theoretical and practical aspects of the fishing trade: boat maintenance, net repair, sorting and cleaning fish and shellfish, and odd jobs in the freezing and shrimp processing plants. The ultimate goal of the programme is for them to find a job, helping their integration into society. When the

The careening site

Un petit matin
tenté à la criée
de crevettes.
Triée en fonction de
leur calibre, elles sont
achetées par des chinois puis
exportées dans des camions
frigorifiques.

A prawn auction. The imperturbable Chinaman does his sums on his calculator, announces a price and pays the fisherman, while the next catch is thrown onto the pontoon and quickly sorted. The prawns are then refrigerated and exported to Hong Kong or Singapore.

where the trawlers are repaired and repainted in bright colours.

The centre is constructed on a pontoon. A shed serves as a warehouse and repair shop. Two huts are used as a classroom and dormitory, where the children sleep on the floor.

The express boats that ply between Sihanoukville, Thailand and Viêt Nam, Cambodia's two great neighbours.

The children are waiting for us around the car. They're delighted to see Benito again and curious about our presence. Benito jokes with them; he knows them all by their first names and introduces us to those he has seen grow up.

weather prevents them going to sea, the youngsters—penniless from spending their wages immediately—are sometimes tempted by some petty theft or an illicit deal. Crime is endemic in the area. In fact Sihanoukville is controlled by one of the country's most powerful mafias, and it's hard for these boys, who have neither ID nor social status, to stay out of trouble. The conversation at lunch revolves around their latest escapades, which are causing Krousar Thmey some problems. "Four of them came up with a plan: they stole wallets on the beach for a gang leader, who happened to be a policeman. Normally the boss takes his cut before sharing out the rest. Except this time, the policeman took off with all the money. Furious, the boys ambushed him as he was leaving a club but didn't just beat him up; they also wrecked his motorcycle. A serious mistake. The policeman lodged a complaint, not for himself, but for the bike. The four were thrown into jail for an indeterminate period." In this type of situation, Krousar Thmey's position is extremely difficult: the policeman asked them to pay for the motorcycle in exchange for releasing the children. This seems a little unfair, as the police were also involved, and it is dangerous, because agreeing to pay means a complicity in the system. Strictly speaking the youngsters are independent and as adults they should take responsibility for their actions, so Krousar Thmey refused to pay.

Nevertheless, Benito wonders about their situation in prison: "does anyone have any news? Are they ill? Can we take them food?" Cambodian detainees are a little like those in *Midnight Express*: They are overcrowded, under-fed, bullied by others and suffer from malaria, amoebic dysentery or, worse, cholera—some never make it.

We leave the fishing village for a tour of Sihanoukville by night. Hotels, karaoke bars and casinos have sprung up like mushrooms. Everything has been built, a kind of architectural anarchy, for cheap mass tourism. These enormous cardboard buildings seem to be deserted and

I wonder why. "Wait for the weekend," Benito tells me, "you'll see throngs of Cambodian families arrive. During the day, they all picnic at the beach, and there's a pretty good atmosphere." The clients at the large hotels and casinos are mostly wealthy Chinese and Thai tourists; there are not many Westerners yet, except for a few backpackers. The flip side of all this is that drugs and prostitution are rife and AIDS is now decimating the population of Sihanoukville.

A row of plastic stools wait for clients along the pavements on the main street. Aluminium bowls are filled with strange, gelatinous, sticky things, a mysterious assortment of desserts and delicacies. Benito buys some apples and oranges to give to the youngsters tomorrow.

We can't make a move without being surrounded by a group of children, with arms outstretched and pleading looks, begging. An exhausted, tiny baby is balanced on a young girl's hip. A few metres away, seated on the ground, the mother is breast feeding another.

Damien switches on the bathroom light over the basin and jumps. He was not expecting to come nose to nose with a magnificent orange frog clinging to the mirror. We didn't think to bring earplugs, so we drift in and out of sleep. The night's entertainment starts with dogs barking, followed by cocks crowing at three in the morning, and, at four, the neighbour who spends ages trying to start his car.

Of all these mysterious desserts, I only recognise the fine vermicelli, sticky rice and candied fruits and beans.

SIHANOUKVILLE - MOV 2001

EN SIROTANT UNE ANGKOR BEER BIEN FRAICHE

CAMBODGE

On the beach, attractive
and graceful young
Vietnamese girls carry
heavy platters of fruit
that they sell individually,
then delicately peel
and cut before
presenting
them to us
on a large
banana leaf.

41

8ʰ 15 du matin.

Wednesday, 28ᵗʰ November

We wake up at six. The sun is already up and the sky is clear. There's no shower, so to wash we scoop up bowlfuls of water from a huge glazed jar, sluicing ourselves down.

Benito places two bolts of red and blue checked material on the table and asks me to choose my favourite. I opt for the red. He takes a pair of scissors and cuts three pieces, all the same size. "The true traditional cotton kramas are sold in rolls; all the others, sold individually, are acrylic or polyester. You can tell it's cotton by touching it, but tourists don't like the stiffness. They have to be washed several times to remove the starch before becoming soft." Benito dips our kramas in soap, washes and rinses them twice, twists them and they are almost dry, ready to wear when we leave for the port.

Monsieur Pech Bin is waiting in front of the trawler with the boys we saw yesterday and I notice a few new faces too. While Benito distributes the fruit, I spot an adolescent, hunched over, walking with a terrible limp. Benito whispers that he has just been let out of prison. He's not at all handicapped, but the inmates are packed tightly together and there's little space to exercise. When they get out, their muscles are so atrophied that it takes them a while to unwind and recover their mobility.

The trawler heads straight across the bay, towards a group of islands. As soon as we have gone past the last jetty, the sea gets rougher and I feel seasick. I give up my drawing and lie down. Damien is getting seriously sunburned on his forehead and nose. We have all tied our kramas around our heads to prevent sunstroke.

Kronsar Thmey has two trawlers, which are used to teach fishing skills to teenagers from the streets of Phnom Penh. Four of them go with us on our excursion to a little island. They laugh and joke with Benito. Only one of them keeps quiet and seems to want to hide his emaciated face under his sunhat. He's just come out of prison.

Everyone is cracking jokes and laughing except for Monsieur Pech Bin, who remains imperturbable. Nothing seems to surprise him, his face remaining impassive and inscrutable since our arrival. The trawler slows down and we drop anchor in a small cove. Benito and one of the youngsters immediately dive overboard. We all follow suit. I let myself float in the wonderful crystal-clear water, my nausea disappearing instantly.

On the Road to Siem Reap

They sleep, mouths half-open, heads resting against the wall or buried in a cushion...

Thursday, 29th November
The centre for street children, Phnom Penh

Justin, busy until now with a reportage in Turkey, joins us this morning. He barely has time to change and take a shower before we drop him in at the deep end, in the centre of Phnom Penh.

We are in the Psar Depot area. The pavement is littered with spare engine parts, exhaust pipes, tyres and truck axles. The house for the street children, a two-storey building with a small courtyard, sits amid all this scrap-metal. A man and a woman greet us with deference as we arrive. I am struck by the calm of the place. Where are the children? I can see rows of mini flip-flops arranged at the foot of the staircase, but I can't hear the normal hubbub. It's eleven in the morning, the children have just been given a snack and they're resting upstairs. The majority spend most of the night in the streets of Phnom Penh, and they often arrive at the centre hungry and exhausted. On tiptoe we climb the stairs and, in the confined space, stand at the edge of the mats, gazing on the mass of small bodies curled up and nestled deep under the covers. In sleep some of the children are so intertwined that we can't tell which arm or leg belongs to whom. Feet stick out from under the blankets, their pink toes resembling tiny vulnerable puppets.

ថ្ងៃនេះ តើខ្ញុំបានធ្វើអំពើល្អវិខ្លះ ?

... like babies who
instinctively keep
to the edge of
their cradles,
trying to get
back to the
protective
environment
of the womb.

"Psar Tuol Tom Pong" or Russian market[6]

Benito has to buy a few things before we leave for Siem Reap. We rush over to the Russian market, which closes at 5pm on the dot. It's a treasure trove, and a favourite among expatriates and tourists. They come here to buy souvenirs, real and fake antiques, jewellery, silk, CDs and DVDs for two or three dollars. They can also find locally made brand-name clothing for next to nothing. The passageways are suffocatingly narrow and poorly lit with neon lights, but the place is exciting and totally magical. While Justin looks through the CDs, Damien takes me to find a road map and, hoping to take a shortcut, we end up amongst the hardware and tools. We walk to the next alley and we're in the middle of a sweatshop: some forty-odd women, hunched over their work, are sewing at breakneck speed on antique machines. We finally find Benito again at a silk stall, where he is selecting scarves, stoles and kramas.

End of the shift

On the outskirts of town we drive past the textile factories. Night is starting to fall. The greenish glare of neon signs illuminates the gates that are barricaded as tightly as fortresses. People crowd around the entrances. The day shift is over and the night shift is about to begin. Open trucks are waiting to take the workers home. Public transportation doesn't exist, hence the large number of makeshift collective taxis, like these scooters trailing carts. Several drive past loaded with female workers. They are seated in rows, their legs dangling over the sides, squeezed in tightly against each other. Their body language expresses total resignation and fatigue. Aged between sixteen and twenty-five, they look prematurely old. They are taken like cattle to their lodgings. These they share with two or three other girls to ease the rent, which, at 20 dollars per month, is too high— they earn only 40 or 50 dollars working a seven-day week. Their families

The "Psar Thol Tom Pong" OR Russian Market.

UNIQUE GAS

46

the art of
concentrating
a maximum
of goods in
a minimum
of space!

usually live far away and they're not always given the two-week holiday, stipulated by law, to go home to visit. When a large order comes in, they have to work day and night. If, however, the factory slows down they are laid off indefinitely without warning or pay. Nevertheless, most of these girls come from rural areas and consider themselves lucky to have found work, despite the terrifying working conditions.

The large European and American designers have their clothes made here, and in neighbouring countries, with mystifyingly ironic names painted large on the front gates: "Eternity", "Gaiety Clothes Factory", "Harmony Apparel Factory".

Friday, 30th November
From Phnom Penh to Siem Reap

We leave at dawn, five of us in the 4x4. Damien and Justin are in the back with the luggage, on the "bumbruiser" seats. Benito is driving, while I share the front seat with Patrick. The road is still fairly smooth yet we already feel overcrowded and jostled. It doesn't bode well for the rest of the trip, ahead is a long day's travel in the heat and dust: it will take us over twelve hours, including stops, to cover the 311 kilometres separating Phnom Penh from Siem Reap.

We leave the capital by the north-east, crossing the Tonle Sap River on the Chroy Chengvar "Japanese friendship" bridge, so named as it was reconstructed by the Japanese after the Khmer Rouge bombed in it 1973. This time, it's the billboards that attract my attention. It doesn't matter if they're modern and European-looking, or painted in some kitsch retro style, there's always an amusing or quirky detail that catches your eye. The one for Alain Delon cigarettes, for example, praises "The taste of France" and is illustrated by a series of photos of the actor in ridiculously sentimental situations. In an entirely different vein, another one uses naive propaganda-like imagery to illustrate an enormous bear being chopped to

47

On the back
of a bus,
Alain Delon
cigarettes

vaunt
"The taste
of France".

↑ le n3 qui sèche
au bord de la route
Sud des maltées.

Patrick, dandy
pacifist and
vegetarian,

comes with us
on the road
to Siem Reap.

pieces with hatchets and knives. Blood spurts out everywhere and the wounds are painted with the precision of a medical textbook. I'm not dreaming: the poster is actually pleading for the protection of animals. This might be funny in another country, but here, where not so long ago humans tortured and massacred each other, it's horrific and I can't bear to look at it.

2001, Cambodia: How is it possible not to think about it all the time? Is it just a Western obsession, with a distorted view of its own civilisation? I can't stop asking myself: How do they manage? How can they live with such a violent past? Today the people of my generation, between thirty-five and forty years old, form the governing class of Cambodia; yesterday they were all either victims or responsible for the atrocities. Now they live, work and eat together. Yet there have been no war-crimes trials, no purging of the collective memory, nothing to exorcise the ghosts of the past. I haven't been here very long, but already the country and the people have charmed me. One big radiant smile sums them up. Rarely in all my travels have I been greeted with so much kindness, so freely and sincerely expressed. It is a generalisation, of course, and may be superficial, but until now, the faces I've seen all reflect an overwhelming "joie de vivre", both in the city and the countryside. I want to forget everything I've read or heard about Cambodia, setting aside my prejudices. I'd like to be spontaneous and open-minded, at least for the duration of this trip.

It's early and the light is still soft. From the car window I watch peaceful countryside scenes unfold: the unchanging, ancestral rituals of farmers working in the fields, stroking their oxen's necks as they pull a cart, and of women replanting rice, bending over the tightly spaced rows of young shoots, their faces hidden by the pointed cones of their hats. There's a lot of traffic and the trucks look seriously overloaded. They are transporting two or three tons more than the authorised amount. With enormous potholes everywhere, deep ruts and perpetual clouds of dust created by the heavy traffic, the

A Khmer on a bicycle, with bamboo stems full of palm wine strapped to his luggage rack.

One of the painted posters denouncing the traffic of animals.

The "thnôt", or sugar palm, is rather like

the national tree, guardian of the rice paddies.

catching glistening strands of

aquatic grasses as they pass...

Boats slide languorously across the water,

road is truly catastrophic. Even so, the trucks, motor-cycles and cars keep up a fairly good speed, knowing every inch of the road.

Skun is the first large town we pass through. Benito parks the car. A swarm of pavement sellers immediately runs towards us carrying round, woven platters piled high with enormous black spiders, all of which have been grilled and lacquered. The girls offering these disgusting-looking things don't seem to realise that they have no chance whatsoever of selling us any. I may have eaten grilled grasshoppers in the Sahara, but my culinary curiosity stops there. And "no, really!" stuffed turtles don't tempt me either. They certainly look pretty, with their shiny curved shells, but my appetite has just been ruined.

It's late morning now and the children are coming home from school, walking in small groups along the road. They're wearing navy blue and white uniforms and all have jolly, bright-coloured Chinese backpacks. Eagerly they head toward a tiny hand-pulled cart. It's carrying a chunk of ice, a grater, a box filled with sticks and three bottles of syrup. A mother hands the vendor a bill and he delicately prepares his concoction. He grates the ice, which he then packs into a cornet with a wooden stick. As a wonderful final gesture, he pours a stream of red, yellow and then green syrup over his ephemeral sculpture. The ice cone is ready to eat! Patrick, enchanted by the sight and moved by the crowd of happy-looking children, gives the man two dollars to make some for the entire group. Benito bursts out laughing as we drive away: "With what you've given him, he could make eighty ice cones at least, not just fifteen. That's a day's wages!"

We overtake a scooter dragging an endless thorny branch. Benito explains the purpose of this bamboo pole. It is used as a ladder to climb the sugar palm trees in the

Palmier à sucre.

morning and at night, when the sap is most abundant. After cutting the stem of the flower, the sap is collected in the dry, hollow stems of bamboo. This is a dangerous and hard job, it's poorly paid and only performed by landless peasants who have no other means of subsistence. At one time, these tree climbers were considered so lowly they didn't even have to pay taxes. The thnôt, the sugar palm, is something of a national tree and is associated with the rice paddies, usually being planted along their embankments. We reach Kompong Thom, the halfway point, and have lunch in a Chinese restaurant where Benito often stops. He orders soup with all sorts of odd floating things in it, and some fried rice and vegetables for Patrick, who's a vegetarian. He advises us to clean our bowls, glasses and chopsticks carefully, with tissues, before eating. Two televisions are broadcasting the news on CNN about Afghan mullahs. It looks as out of place to us as if we were looking at pictures from Mars. We don't have time to visit the city but Benito wants to show us the few old colonial buildings that remain in this provincial town. Damien begs us to let him take one last photograph near the bridge. When he doesn't re-appear Benito becomes impatient. The latter is like a supercharged battery and has a hard time adapting to the nonchalant "happy-go-lucky" rhythm of our Damiano, whom we grab in the middle of the bridge, waving a few polaroids. He'd come across three children, one stark naked, diving into the Sen River.

On the outskirts of Kompong Thom we take a detour to see Sambot Prei Kuk[7], a pre-Angkor city, where some of the oldest temples in Cambodia are to be found. There are supposedly more than one hundred of them scattered through the forest. We limit ourselves to a brief stroll around Ishanapura, where the vegetation is slowly eating away at several brick structures. Having not yet seen the

Intrepid
divers on the
bridge of
the river "Sen".

MILD SEVEN

ស័ម្ពូ ព្រៃគុក
SAM BOR PREI KUK

Half-way, a signpost
indicates the site of
Sambor Prei Kuk,
the preangkorian town.

A villa from the colonial era, whose structure continues to resist the passing of time.

splendours of Angkor, we are already excited by the unique feel of discovering dilapidated blocks of stone, forgotten for centuries. There's no one here, apart from two guards stationed in a hut. One of them stirs from his drowsiness just long enough to guide us around. A herd of cows ambles around the stones, overseen by three mischievous children, who play hide-and-seek with us.

We are still far from Siem Reap and the road is getting much worse. Benito, however, accelerates, as he doesn't want to drive at night. The dust already restricts the visibility, but after dark it's like driving blind. Many cars don't even have headlights. The light outside is magnificent and transforms the countryside we're driving through. It's now the time for bathing and fishing: the surface of the water is dotted with small shiny heads. The children are having a great time, laughing and splashing, while remaining a respectful distance from the fishermen. These men wade through the water, waist-high, trying to find the best spot. When they do they cast their nets wide into the air, the tiny droplets of water glistening in the evening sun.

Benito speeds up even more. He absolutely wants us to see the Kompong Kdei bridge[8], one of the most beau-tiful from the Angkor period, sixty-five kilometres south-east of Siem Reap. By the time we reach it the bridge has already turned bluish in the dusk; however, there's enough light to make out the tall narrow arches made of red laterite[9]. The hoods of the Nagas[10], the seven-headed mythical snakes guarding either side of the bridge, are still intact. I sketch them, but it's too late for the colour, and the deep red of the laterite has already faded. Beside me, Patrick is talking with a foreigner. If I dared, I'd ask him for his mobile phone to call Trappes for news of Garance. For the first time since our arrival I miss her. She's not yet two years old and we've never been away from her. We haven't been able to get in touch with our families and suddenly I'm worried, imagining all the things that could happen to her. Patrick must have felt something, as he asks me if I'm "alright?" He understands instinctively, even before I answer, and hands me the phone, saying, "Here, call your daughter!"

Suddenly it's pitch black. Three times on the side of the road, we see scenes from the life of Jesus projected upon screens stretched between two trees: "It's those evangelist missionaries again," concludes Benito.

The laterite bridge of Kompong Kdei, the only one that has survived from the Angkorian age.

La cité pré-Angkorienne de Sambor Prey Kuk

The tonffalo loves ponds and can spend many a happy how there. From time to time he lifts his muzzle to sniff the air.

Saturday, 1st December
Day One at Angkor

It's 6:45am when we leave Borann, l'Auberge des Temples, to drive to the City of the Gods. This is a big day: we've been waiting for, and dreaming about, this moment for such a long time. On the way we discover Siem Reap. The small town is attractive and well kept, and has become one of the most popular tourist destinations in Southeast Asia. Just five years ago, there were hardly any hotels and no streets lights in the deserted avenues. As we cross the bridge, we turn right at a roundabout dominated by a giant portrait of the king and queen in an ornate gilt frame. We drive alongside the Grand Hotel and its gardens and head straight, driving the five kilometres to the entrance of the site. Nothing is closed off. The temples are all open to the Cambodian families who inhabit the edge of the fabulous surrounding forest, in their wooden or latania-leaf houses. Other than bird song the shrilling of insects envelops us. The place is alive and the stone feels inhabited. We have finally reached the sacred realm.

Constructed by a lineage of Khmer kings, the temples of Angkor are the result of an exceptional civilisation, that once stretched from Burma to the Mekong Delta. It appeared during the era of Alexander the Great, when Indian navigators travelled here and settled by the river, trading peaceably with the indigenous peoples. The newcomers introduced their gods: Brahma[11], Shiva[12], Vishnu[13], as well as the epic legends of the Ramayana[14]. The masters of

this newly founded kingdom constructed gigantic and beautifully sculpted temples, of which Angkor Wat is the undisputed masterpiece.

The Khmer civilisation had reached the peak of its power and glory in the eleventh and twelfth centuries, before it declined, undermined by the conflicts of succession and other internecine warfare. The magnificent city was invaded, brutally sacked and set ablaze by the Chams[15] in 1177. King Jayavarman VII expelled the invaders and re-conquered his throne. He broke away from Hindu traditions and converted his people to a new god, Buddha, constructing a sumptuous city called Angkor Thom. The city's temples were built in homage to the incarnation of the God King, whose message was one of detachment and compassion. The Khmer empire then mysteriously and rapidly declined, the temples disappearing beneath the jungle for four centuries.

In the mid-nineteenth century, the French naturalist Henri Mouhot came in search of a beetle and stumbled upon this incredible site by chance. Since then, researchers, archaeologists, architects and restorers have poured into the region, working under the direction of the École Française d'Extrême-Orient (EFEO). For more than one hundred years all have contributed to the renaissance and reconstruction of Angkor.

The grandeur of the site is overwhelming: more than 200 temples are scattered over an area of approximately 40 square kilometres. The largest, Angkor Wat, forms a vast rectangle of one square kilometre, with a perimeter of 8 by 2 kilometres. Benito suggests that we start with the medium-sized temples and work our way up to Angkor Wat. The temple of Banteay[16] Kdei will be the first we visit.

Banteay Kdei

Located north-east of Angkor Wat, Banteay Kdei faces a magnificent ornamental lake, the Srah[17] Srang. Balustrades decorated with Nagas and lions are interspersed on a landing platform, whose steps disappear beneath the

In their grey-blue uniforms, the Apsara guards blend into the background.

One of the little girls who sell carved bamboo flutes, bracelets and toys.

The "gopuras" are gigantic entrance portals, topped with a four-sided face of Buddha.

water. Benito tells us that the Khmer Rouge used the sacred lake as a common grave, throwing the bodies of their victims into it. Children play on the road, waiting for the next tourist they can assail: "sum waterrr, misterr, buyyy mee somethiiiing... three flutes for one dollaaa, madaamm." They offer film, postcards, cans of water and CocaCola, bamboo flutes in woven sheathes, bracelets and other trinkets. Despite the hordes of tourists every day the children retain their spontaneity and seem naturally kind. Surprised to hear Benito speaking Khmer, they give him a woven willow bracelet.

We walk towards the gate of Banteay Kdei, extremely moved at the sight. The head of a Buddha with four faces overlooks the entrance, almond-shaped eyes gazing out from the four cardinal points. Carved directly from a pile of stone blocks, the curved features are striated with irregular thin cracks, the edges of each cube of sandstone. Over time nature has eroded the surface of the stone, which is also covered with moss and lichen in places. This juxtaposition of textures and colours seems to bring the sculptures to life. I could linger for a long time around this immense gate, exploring each tiny detail of the exquisite feminine figures, the Devatas[18], nestled in the hollow of niches surrounded by carved decorative friezes. I am overcome by the perfection

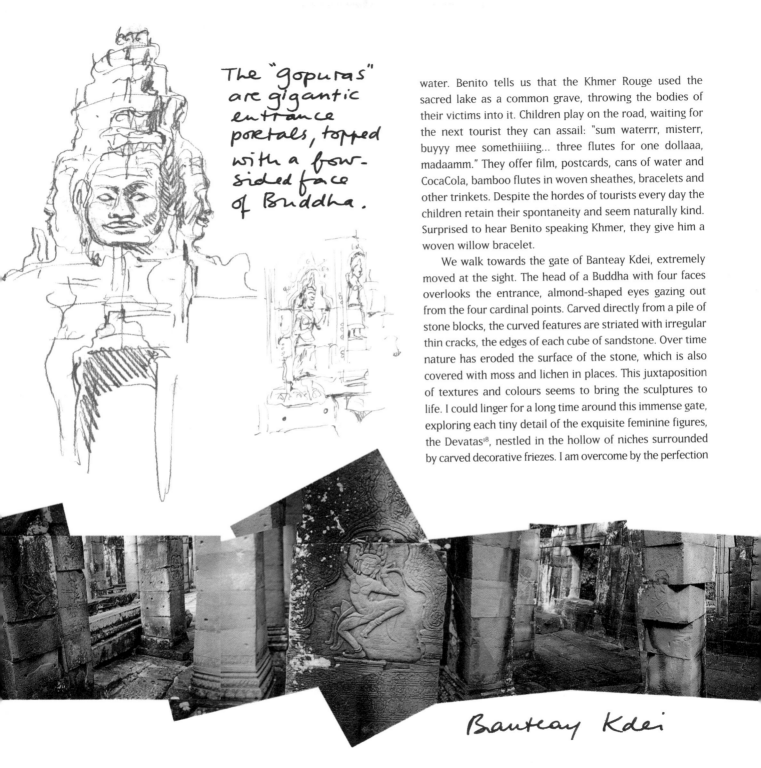

Banteay Kdei

At the western facade of Banteay kdei, a giant kapok tree, whose trunk shines like gold, spreads its roots like tentacles.
Sitting on the ground, I disturb a colony of a ants that chase me away, biting my ankles and calves.

and the disturbing sensuality of their gentle expressive faces, their curved breasts and their tiny waists broadening into smooth stomachs, cinched by a belt supporting floral sarongs. After a few minutes, I tear myself away from this first vision, which is only a foretaste of the wonders that wait at the end of the path.

The entrance to the sanctuary is dappled with sunlight filtering through the branches overhead. With restraint, slowing every footstep, I tread the path leading to the first galleries, motivated by an instinctive desire to blend with the decor, the better to understand it. I step over loose blocks of stone on the threshold of the first Gopura[19]. I peer straight into a narrow, seemingly endless central corridor and suddenly realise the impressive length of this temple. The fairly reasonable size of the entrance gives no idea of the extent of the labyrinth of corridors, leading to countless rooms in which statues and other mythic representations are still worshipped. I know nothing about how these temples were constructed or the rules which governed the layout of the libraries, the dance rooms and various spaces, around the central sanctuary consisting of a group of towers, each carved with the enigmatic faces,

ANGKOR - Nov 2001

TA PROHM, À L'ÉCART DES TOURISTES -

Ta Phrom was a Buddhist monastery built between the twelfth and thirteenth centuries in the middle of a 60 hectare enclosure. 12640 people lived there, including 18 high priests, 2740 officiant priests, 1617 assistants and 615 dancers.

Hordes of tourists follow one other, obeying their guide, who indicates the precise spot, to the nearest centimetre, where photos should be taken.

Ta Phrom is one of the only temples left in its "natural state" by the EFEO, no doubt because it has fused with the jungle to an extraordinary degree. The roots of kapok trees and ficus have the ruins in such a tight grip that trying to remove them would be tantamount to destroying the entire construction.

This old man, tirelessly sweeping the inner courtyards of Ta Phrom, has become inseperable from the temple where he's taken up Residence.

He's to be found in most of the books and guides on Angkor, a slight figure in the corners of a photo.

Over time these designs changed with the successive sovereigns of Angkor. I suddenly feel dizzy. No matter which way I look, each view is captivating and breathtakingly beautiful. The columns are all decorated with highly detailed motifs, delicate friezes of dancing Apsaras[20] alternating with rows of Devatas set in alcoves.

I leave Damien and Justin behind, who are probably trying, unsuccessfully, to take photographs. I hurry forward, trying to avoid the moment that I have to confront the blank page. How can I draw perfection, the sublime! No line could truly capture the curve of a cheek, the subtlety of a smile, the nuance of a gaze. I am in a state of shock. I chuckle as I read in a guide that "Banteay Kdei retains what Maurice Glaize[21] called 'the spirit of confusion' that runs throughout the works of Jayavarman VII." Confusion! The word is perfect to describe my state of mind. Two hours have gone by in a flash, and I haven't even reached the western entrance of the wall surrounding the temple. How are we going to "produce" drawings and photographs? It's a challenge that tempers my delight. Still confused, I meet up with Justin and Damien, who are struck with the same doubts.

Sunday, 2nd December
Sunrise over Angkor Wat

The alarm goes off at 4:40am. It's pitch black outside, but we want to be among the first to watch the sun rise over Angkor[22] Wat, the largest and the most extraordinary of all the Khmer temples. It is aptly named the "city that became a pagoda". We are not the only ones rushing to the temples this early in the morning.

Although it's still dark, there's already something of a festival feeling at the site. A platform and some tarpaulins have been set up on either side of the causeway. Loudspeakers are blaring out aggressive music that's hard on the ear. I had hoped for a more tranquil atmosphere.

During the night, I had forgotten about the marathon and the runners who will cross the finishing line at this

5:30 am : a Buddhist ceremony celebrating the full moon oR, maybe, the promise of dawn over Angkor Wat.

very spot in less than four hours' time. Small groups of tourists have formed. Still and silent, they have decided to wait for the sudden panoramic view of the five towers of Angkor at sunrise, silhouetted against the lightening sky. We are too impatient, and decide instead to take on this giant and be the first to scale the steep pyramidal steps. An unfamiliar ceremony is taking place on the esplanade as we arrive. Monks and other worshippers have spread mats at the base of stalls decked with yellow and pink umbrellas. These movable, decorated altars are heavily laden with offerings. Worshippers with shaved heads, simply dressed in white as servants of Buddha, move constantly between the praying monks and the altars, re-lighting sputtering candles and re-arranging offerings. In contrast with their elders, who are able to distance themselves from the real world instantaneously, the novice monks are wide-eyed and gaze cheekily at the rows of tourists watching their every move. One of them glances curiously at my drawing as he mechanically tosses flower petals. The beauty of the moment lies in the subtle mix of seriousness and innocence.

It's now six in the morning and the entrance to Angkor Wat is finally open. We rush forward, following Benito, walking straight past the long series of corridors, arches and doorways, where meditative Buddhas still sleep, and almost run to the base of the central structure, a temple mountain rising above an immense terrace. It symbolises Mount Meru, the centre of the universe for Buddhists. A single steep set of stairs on the south side leads to the top. I climb the steps one by one, without looking down, as I'm afraid of heights. Once I reach the top of this pyramid, I discover cloisters and galleries linking the four corner towers and the central tower. This is the sanctuary that housed the statue of the God-King in the form of Vishnu before it was stolen. As daylight arrives I gradually see, emerging from the bluish darkness, seven notched and ribbed rings, one upon another, curving upwards to the

In the gallery of "bas-reliefs", thousands of pilgrims' hands have polished the sandstone, turning the alabaster hue into a black laquer.

top, which is formed by three rows of lotus petals. The symbolic number seven represents the seven circles of Mount Meru, which dominates three terraces that in turn represent the elements—earth, wind and water—the essential components of the cosmic mountain. All being surrounded by the moats, representing the ocean. I sit down on the edge of a small terrace under one of the corner towers. There are not many of us at this height: just a few backpackers and worshippers, busy with their morning prayers around the divinities. Damien, Patrick, Benito and Justin are all seated around me. They are quiet, enjoying the silence and the privilege of being in the front row for the spectacle that's about to unfold. Suddenly the burnished sun rises, waking the sleeping beauty, as rays of pearled light illuminate every detail, slowly warming the pale shades of gold and pink sandstone, creating a shimmering saffron yellow as bright as that of the monks' robes. We remain seated a long time, transfixed by the monumental beauty of the architecture, seen at its very best with the rising sun setting off each and every detail.

After our collective meditation, we separate and I continue my walk alone, looking for the famous gallery of bas-reliefs. As opposed to the central temple reserved for sovereigns, priests and dancers, this gallery was open to all worshippers, depicting for them the various episodes of the legend of Vishnu, in a long frieze running around the four walls of the temple. Even before discovering the first bas-reliefs, I am struck by the classicism and elegance of this clear and continuous line, bordered by columns that filter the sunlight. But most of all I can't believe I'm alone, infinitely small and fragile, as before my eyes scenes of historic battles, sumptuous ceremonies and legendary, epic myths unfold on this fresco, measuring two metres high by six hundred metres long. I wander through this universe packed with thousands of details, incapable of understanding the meaning of the multiple and frenetic combats, despite explanations from the guidebook.

The gallery is lined with a collection of statues of Buddha - often sadly mutilated or decapitated.

In the distance, I spot two figures that stand out in the doorway of one of the corner pavilions, and I suddenly feel like following them.

The roadway is swarming with people now. Justin chats with two young monks; the elder tells him he'd like to change his life, get a real job and earn some money. He's tired of living off other people and of the passivity imposed by the religion. He's an orphan, who was entrusted to the pagoda at the age of six, so it was natural that he should then become a monk. But there's no obligation to wear the robes for life!

We reluctantly leave Angkor Wat, aware that we've only seen a tiny part of it. We'll be back.

10 - Les ruines d'Angkor - P. N.

In principle, every Cambodian must don the saffron robe for at least a few months at some stage in his life. Despite being optional, the rule is widely respected.

71

Then I walk past two local families and monks, pleasantly surprised to see that Angkor is still a holy place and is widely visited by Cambodians, especially at weekends, when entire families and groups make pilgrimages here, or simply come for a Sunday picnic. In the distance I catch sight of two figures standing out against one of the corner buildings and I decide to follow them. They are moving so gracefully, the wind raising the loose ends of their draped robes, but I lose them as they disappear behind a corner on the north side, as fleeting as butterflies. I run to try to catch up with them, but when I turn the corner I discover only a deserted corridor. What secret passageway did they use to disappear so quickly? My eyes are tired, I'm hungry and I can't concentrate on the profusion of bas-reliefs that are starting to blur together. Is it because I am alone that I'm so sensitive to the spookiness of the atmosphere? Is that what troubles me so? I have to sit down, feeling suddenly dizzy. Children's voices, like small clanging crystal balls, swirl around inside my head. I no longer have the strength to move; sounds, sights, everything is getting confused. The boys have set out to look for me and arrive just at this moment to rescue me from this strange lethargy. We have been up for five hours; all we want now is a swim in the pool and a hearty lunch.

A chorus of shouts and applause interrupts our discussion with the monks.

the marathon runners cross the finishing line and the winners are cheered.

អំណោយរបស់ ក្រុមហ៊ុនស្រាបៀរ កម្ពុជា

A COMMUNITY PROJECT BY CAMBREW

TONLE SAP

BALLADE SUR LE TONLÉ SAP –

After helping his father to start the engine, the taciturn teenager sulks at the front of the boat as it slaloms through the flooded forest.

Sunday, 2nd December
Lake dwellers

The village of Chong Knea, known as the "floating Vietnamese village", extends from either side of a packed-earth causeway that gradually descends into the lake. Following the seasonal rising and falling of the water the entire village moves along this strip. Depending on their origins—Cambodian, Cham, Chinese or Vietnamese—the villagers live in houses built on stilts, shacks floating on empty oilcans or boats transformed into living spaces. Moored to the causeway, they set up temporary huts from which they run their businesses. As we leave, we watch the arrival of the sleek steel express boat that runs from Phnom Penh to Siem Reap in five hours. A horde of "coolies" are busy on the deck grabbing the various bags belonging to tourists, while these same disoriented tourists grasp the railings.

Benito has rented a small motorboat at the Phnom Khrom jetty. It has an awning, along with wicker seats with padded cushions. On each seat is a life jacket. We hustle our way down this main street to our boat, led by an old man and a taciturn young boy. The young boy pushes on a long bamboo pole, the boat gliding out over the surface of the water. The motor then splutters to life, and we roar off for a few hundred metres before settling to a more comfortable cruising speed. The landscape

We meet several fishermen, who perform a subtle dance routine, half-aquatic, half-aerial, when casting their nets.

changes completely. We slalom through a flooded forest, wending our way among the tops of mangrove trees sticking out of the water. The wake of the boat rustles the branches, disturbing herons, kingfishers and even storks and pelicans that take flight. We motor past dugouts carved from single tree trunks, their ram-like bows stretching out over the water. We follow a network of fishing nets, running alongside the pruol, a system of dams and enclosures that trap the fish but also act as breeding reservoirs. The fishing techniques vary with the seasons and hence the water levels. According to a local expression, to fish you need either a shovel or a ladder. As the water constantly either rises or falls, the fish can sometimes be dug from the mud or plucked from the trees. This proverb is not far from the truth: in the lake there are certain "black" fish that can live both in and out of the water. You see them crawling across roads from one ricepaddy to another, using their fins as little levers. They can live for weeks under a crust of dried mud, surviving on their own reserves.

A very strange craft is floating towards us; Justin nicknames it the "praying mantis". A huge funnel-shaped basket, trailing a net stretched by the force of the current between two sampans, hangs down from two poles sticking out from the bow like the antennae of a giant insect. This technique is used from November to January, as the water starts to recede, the catch being particularly abundant during full moon. Fishermen prize especially the small fish. These are named "riels", after the Cambodian currency, and are sold to make prahoc, the ubiquitous fermented fish paste, sometimes jokingly called "Cambodian cheese" for its strong smell. Everyone works to prepare it; removing heads, trampling the fish in wicker baskets, then salting them before leaving the mixture to ferment in large wooden barrels. The prahoc thus produced provides Cambodians with a valuable source of protein throughout the year.

The lakeside village of Kompoong Phenk.
The main street is flooded. According to
the level of the lake, the inhabitants of
the houses on stilts dismantle their walls
to move to the upper floor, which is
sometimes over 7 metres high.

By the pagoda, Justin has met a distinguished old man, whom he thinks is the spitting image of Ryu Chishu, the favorite actor of Japanese filmmaker Ozu.

As I draw him, I notice a detail that fascinates me: his ears are like those of Buddha. They are three times bigger than ours, perfectly rounded and delicately rimmed, and they taper towards the lobe, hanging like a drop of falling water.

Isolated in the middle of this immense natural reserve, the village of Kompong Phluk finally appears. All the fishermen from this village are Khmer as opposed to most of them on the lake who are Vietnamese. Being built on stilts, their houses are radically different from the floating houses. According to the level of the lake, the house, constructed from movable panels, can slide up and down the stilts, sometimes to a height of over seven metres. When the level is low the panels can be used to construct a shelter near the water's edge. We moor at the base of a pagoda, the only brick construction, on a spur of land. In the middle of the rainy season, the level of the lake rises more than seven metres and the surface area is multiplied five-fold (from 2,700 square kilometres to almost 15,000 square kilometres, nearly 8 percent of the entire country). Right now, the main street is completely underwater, so we are unable to look around the village.

From the terrace of an unfinished house, we watch small episodes from their daily life, as if in a theatre: clusters of youngsters hang onto ladders and lean on the balustrades. They dive into the water, splashing each other, playing games. Constantly one or two canoes float along this canal, gliding soundlessly over the flooded roadway. I admire all the different ways the women have of tying the kramas covering their heads and faces. Leaning on the railings of their houses, the women call out to the boatmen, selecting the items they want and sending down their baskets. Even the hairdresser visits her customers by boat. The ducks, chickens and pigs are also kept in floating cages.

Justin appears, flanked by a cheerful crowd of children and an elegant old man, whom he found in the pagoda, along with three monks and a dog fast asleep on the floor. The children are pulling Justin by the arm to get him to play football with them. The ball is hardly a ball, just a lump of punctured plastic really. On the bank other children are playing with clay, modelling figures, boats, cars and, strangely, helicopters. They use strips of plastic bags to fashion sails for their boats and clothing for their tiny dolls, while ice-cream sticks become propellers. The trip back by boat is magnificent. The surface of the lake turns silver, shimmering under the slanting rays of the sun. I watch for the streamlined and fleeting shapes of flying fish as they leap out of the water.

The shopkeepers and grocers, who deliver hens, ducks and pigs, and even the hairdresser travel by boat to their clients' homes.

The children crowd around Justin and drag him to come and play football with them. Damien picks up the sweet papers that litter the ground.

79

FROM BANTEAY SREI TO BENG MEALEA

Mao, the one-legged receptionist from
Boraun, fulfils an old dream: to make
a pilgrimage to Beng Mealea.

Monday, 3rd December

We're getting used to rising at four in the morning. Today should be even more exceptional than previous days. Benito is taking us on the "grand tour" to see the most remote temples, particularly Beng Mealea, which is so overgrown by the jungle that it is practically inaccessible. Mao, the one-legged receptionist at Borann, is with us. He has been in Siem Reap for one year now but still hasn't visited Beng Mealea. He's delighted to be able to make this pilgrimage at last. Benito warned him that it would be a rough trip, the road being in a terrible condition, bumpy from start to finish. We will be walking for over an hour in the forest and will visit no fewer than four different sites. Mao just laughs, he's seen worse. A former soldier, he lost his leg twenty years ago when he stepped on a land mine, yet he's so agile and fast on his crutches that we almost forget he's disabled. After working as a translator in the refugee camps, he returned to the country in 1993 and took on a number of small jobs to feed his wife and children. During one of Benito's trips to Battambang, Mao recognised him and asked for a job. A few weeks later he started work at Borann.

Banteay Srei

Located some twenty kilometres north-east of Angkor, towards Phnom Kulen[23], Banteay Srei[24] is one of Benito's favourite temples. Also known as the "citadel of women" it is considered to be the jewel of Khmer art. The sculptures and pediments are carved with a perfection and refinement not seen elsewhere. This unique temple is one of Angkor's smallest, and the only time to fully appreciate it is at dawn, before the first mini-vans start dropping tourists off at 7am. Banteay Srei was constructed in the tenth century by Brahman Yajnavarahale, who was a court advisor to King Rajendravarman. It is still too dark to distinguish the details

Mao has a discreet indigo tattoo on his forehead.

HONG BUNTHORN/ MAO

The sun is just rising, picking out the pink sandstone flecked with greyish-green.

Le lever du jour sur Banteay Srei - Nous sommes seuls dans le temple -

and colour of the temple, constructed entirely from pink sandstone. Patrick is surprised to see a rope cordoning off the central structure, preventing us from seeing the most beautiful door lintels, hidden between the towers and two narrow passageways. The rope was placed there a few months ago, as there were too many tourists for such a small temple. At this early hour the guards are not yet on duty, so we step over the rope to catch, with the aid of a torch, a fleeting vision of the graceful androgynous ephebes intertwined with sensual Devatas. We also catch a glimpse of the choreographed movements of the epic battles between the monkey soldiers and their amazon assistants.

Over the century looters have carried off an incredible number of bas-reliefs and statues, as have museums, finding this to be the best method of forming their collections. André Malraux committed his controversial "crime" in the 1920s at Banteay Srei, when it was still an unknown temple lost deep in the jungle. For some, it was an "unforgivable offence", for others a "youthful error". The romantic young adventurer and his small team tore more than one tonne of sculpted stone from the temple. This exploit landed them in a courtroom in Phnom Penh. The stolen artifacts were returned, but

this didn't prevent the Guimet Museum in Paris from appropriating one of Banteay Srei's most beautiful lintels several years later—via official channels, of course, and for the purposes of archaeological conservation! Banteay Srei was also the site of a particularly successful experiment concerning a restoration technique developed by the Dutch in Java and adopted by the architect-archaeologist Henri Marchal in the 1930s. The results were impressive and he used this technique, called anastylosis[25], on most of the large temples of Angkor, starting with Angkor Wat. Henri Marchal and his staff at the E.F.E.O. accomplished an immense task, working under particularly difficult conditions. They were the real pioneers in the renaissance of Angkor, and are still considered by Cambodians as the "protective spirits" of their cultural heritage.

Kabal Spean, river of "a thousand lingas"

We park at the sandy edge of a forest and take a steep path, with a few handrails and wooden boards here and there, that climbs into the trees. Benito has calculated a good thirty minutes of walking, but Mao doesn't hesitate to follow us and I watch, impressed, as he pulls himself up the path on his crutches, zigzagging among the obstacles

Kabal Spean, whose bed is carved

with a series of "lingas"
and bas-reliefs.

with amazing confidence and flexibility. Under the thick foliage, the air is humid and smells of moss and damp earth. The river appears, winding gently among the rocks. Decorative stone markers line the banks. I look at the riverbed of Kabal Spean[26], searching for the thousand lingas[27] of its name. Damien and Justin have walked ahead and are waiting for me, pointing excitedly at a rock in the water. Sculpted into the riverbed are several "Ophelias", lying for eternity under the stream. The water swirls about their charming faces, splashing over and around them, and sometimes drowning them. Shiny from being constantly wet, they remain smiling, with half-closed eyes. Mao and Benito relax in hammocks left by the riverbank. We try to draw, but without much conviction. This river is one of those natural marvels that you can never really capture.

Beng Mealea

Benito wasn't exaggerating; the road is indeed terrible, and I feel sorry for Damien, Justin and especially Mao, who are even more jostled in the back. We throw up huge clouds of red dust, asphyxiating the many cyclists and people on ox-carts. Scooters are rare in the rural areas far from the main roads. Animals, however, are everywhere: we are constantly avoiding water buffalo, pigs, dogs, ducks, chickens and chicks. Benito stops several times to ask for directions. At the crossings all the roads look alike and he can't remember the way. The last time he came to Beng Mealea he was riding a motorcycle and it was pouring with rain. Today he wonders how he ever reached his destination at all. We have been up since four in the morning and have still not eaten anything. I don't think I can take this interminable road much longer. We finally arrive an hour and a half later. Beng Mealea is an amazing surprise, beyond anything we could have imagined. First of all, its size!

Before being sold at market, the hens undergo a quick beauty treatment after their journey: Their feathers are sprayed with water and a litre or so goes down their throats!

On the Road, Scooters often pass with bundles of at least fifty hens, hanging upside down all the way to the markets, or enormous sows that are tied on their backs, live, to the luggage racks.

In the villages, signs indicate that a pig is available to fertilize the local sows.

ទទួលយកឱកូនគសិករ កើតនៅក្នុងភូមិ មួយ ។ កាលរាយុបាន៧ឆ្នាំ កុមារទទួលយកដែលធំងំនៅ លេងនៅក្បែរផ្ទះលោកស្នេហ៍…។ ថ្ងៃមួយប្រពន្ធស្នេហ៍ឈ្លានញាសំពត់

នៅលើផ្ទះ…ស្រុះត្រូវមកជួ ក្រឡេកឃើញកុមារ ទទួលយកនៅលេងនៅផ្ទះរនោះ ក៏ផ្សែកហៅរោយ ជួយរើសគ្រល់ឱយ…

Try to imagine a temple almost as large as Angkor Wat, entirely overgrown by the jungle, a Babylon where stones, roots and vines are inextricably linked. Mao's trip stops, sadly, at the first wall. All his strength of will and desire are not enough to help him scale this stone monster. Even we wouldn't have been able to find a way in without the help of two young boys who offer to guide us. Mao, however, is not disappointed. He seems happy to be here, delighted to have come this far. He hands us his camera so we can take his picture.

We then start to climb this mountain of stone, sliding through tiny passageways, ending up suddenly in inner courtyards blocked off by other fallen slabs. We pull ourselves up to the top of a wall and stop, amazed at the panorama of all these cloisters, sanctuaries and columns that have withstood the voracious jaws of the vegetation. Looking at this temple, I understand the wonder the discoverers of Angkor must have felt, and I realise the monumental building sites that had to be set up to recover the temples from the jungle and reconstruct them. Each block of stone had to be identified before it could be placed back in its original setting, as in some gigantic puzzle. I am overwhelmed, it only takes Benito to read a few lines by Maurice Glaize to transform me into a heroine from the colonial era. "The excursion to Beng Mealea, which took an entire day, can be combined with a hunt, as the region has much small and large game, and even wild beasts: tigers, panthers and elephants, herds of wild oxen and water buffaloes roam the forest as far as Prah Khan..." I imagine beautiful women, on elephant back, waving their parasols, while their moustachioed men, in ties and pith helmets, shoot at game. I can see them sipping tea, as civilised as can be, in the shade of a banyan tree near one of these temples. Speaking of game, we disturb a highly poisonous snake during our exploration. Our guides move us aside and take on the hissing silver creature, throwing their shoes to stun it

A team of bomb disposal experts works around the temple. Cambodia is still one of the world's most mined countries.

getting to Beng Mealea requires
willpower, patience and
rudimentary climbing
skills.

It's so heavy and humid in the early afternoon that even the children, who are usually so lively and cheerful, are paralysed by the heat.

and then they kill it with stones. As we leave the temple, we come across men clearing land-mines, each one working alone on his assigned plot of land. They are wearing helmets with Plexiglas visors and carry metal detectors, moving slowly around a red pole stuck in the middle of their zone. Time seems to have stopped, frozen by their slow movements and the almost palpable tension. Mine removal is expensive at 1,000 U.S. dollars per mine, and there are several million of them stilll remaining on Cambodian soil. It's painstaking work, especially discouraging when the mine-clearer detects metal and spends as much time removing a nail or a Coke can as he would one of these "eternal sentinels", as the Cambodians call them. The head of the clearance squad politely asks Justin not to take a photograph, explaining that it could distract his men. An accident can happen so quickly. Many European organizations have been pursuing this laudable work for several years now.

Mao is waiting for us under a straw hut, which doubles as a cheap eatery and a chemist-cum-grocer's shop. Next to packets of aspirin and "Number 1" condoms we find some freeze-dried Thai noodles. We have a great meal, washed down with overly sweet litchi juice, but it's exactly what we needed. The heat is stifling, and I have an irresistible urge to sleep.

We're back on the red dirt track, jostling along. We have to get to National Highway 6, fifteen kilometres east of Siem Reap. We pass a couple of men in dungarees on bicycles, who have chiselled features and dark skin. "Typical Khmers Rouges", notes Benito. "You'll see more and more as we go up-country. Their territory extends throughout the entire north-west, along the Thai border, in the forests where they have their camps".

Mao is waiting for us in a straw hut that doubles as a chemist's and grocer's.

Tuesday, 4th December
Leaving for Battambang

We leave Siem Reap for Battambang, Cambodia's second largest city, once famous for its abundant agriculture and gentle lifestyle. The lake is still high enough to allow us to reach it by boat. We leave at dawn, the soft light of the rising sun at our backs. The only drawback on this idyllic morning is the engine, which is unbelievably noisy. I put in earplugs, given that the trip can last from five to eight hours. We're moving at a snail's pace, and we soon have our first breakdown. Fortunately, we're going by one of the floating villages and I take advantage of the moment, stepping over various decrepit pontoons in search of a loo. We take three new passengers aboard, middle-management types with briefcases. My neighbour pulls out some reports and starts scribbling conscientiously. Benito explains that they are civil servants and are certainly on their way to a meeting of the "Cambodian People's Party", the leading Cambodian political party, in anticipation of the February

elections. After crossing the lake and a spectacular ornithological reserve—the Prek Tuol biosphere—we are now travelling through the narrowest canal in the Sangkar River. There are lots of people on the banks, and as we approach Battambang the vegetation changes, as do the houses. The closer we get to Battambang, the more intricate they become. There is more and more rubbish and more plastic objects of all kinds littering the banks, carelessly thrown away. Through the vegetation we can see the gilded towers of pagodas and even the dome of a mosque.

The boat drops us off at our destination, on the banks of the Krousar Thmey school for blind children, built on land donated by King Sihanouk. I am seized by laughter as Benito jumps off the boat onto what I was sure was dry land and sinks in up to his knees in mud. He loses a shoe. The problem is that I can't see any other way off the boat. My hilarity certainly doesn't do much to help me keep my

Departure for Battambang in a covered motor boat.
It coughs, splutters and backfires; thank heavens for my earplugs.

We pass several villages whose houses are floating rather than built on stilts. the entire village moves when the water level rises.

own balance. Nevertheless, I remove my shoes and step off as delicately as possible, but I'm immediately sucked into the mud, and I have the hardest time pulling my legs out of this viscous muck. Justin and Damien escape the ordeal. Benito hands them a plank and they walk off with our bags. Swearing and laughing, we hose our legs down, but the mud won't wash off.

Hearing the noise we made, the children come out of the buildings and head towards us hesitantly, as if they'd lost their sense of balance. We are confronted with the lifeless stares of their little blind faces. Some look at us with milky eyes, in others we can almost detect a pupil. Still others have their eyes glued shut by pus. Yet they smile, revealing all their tiny bad teeth, incredibly happy

that we're here. Half of them, the blind, take courses in Braille, using schoolbooks translated in Cambodia. The others, the deaf, learn in sign language. The children from Battambang and neighbouring towns are brought to school by a system of buses. Those youngsters who live too far away stay here from Monday to Friday, going home at the weekend.

Time is short. We haven't had lunch yet and have to leave for Sisophon, towards the Thai border, this afternoon. We rush through a meal of frogs' legs swimming in fat. The restaurant is deserted and the three waitresses pay us special attention. They constantly bring us more and more ice cubes for our drinks, leering, in fact, at "my men".

Battambang is officially the second largest city in Cambodia after Phnom Penh, and has always been the country's breadbasket. After Siem Reap, we are struck by how peaceful it is, bathed in a provincial charm. Some streets are as lively as those in the capital, the pavements filled with people and goods. Others, however, are deserted at siesta time, seemingly frozen in the 1950s. Strolling along the remaining administrative buildings constructed during King Sihanouk's great modernisation programme, the Sangkum Reastr Niyum[28], we come across roundabouts decorated—not with the traditional six-armed statue of Vishnu—but with massive and determined-looking peasants, arms outstretched, scythe in hand, the

Twenty schoolchildren all stare at us, waving their hands about as they comment on our presence. The teacher translates the nicknames we've just been given. Damien is called "Red nose" because of his sunburn, Justin is "wide face" and for me, the mimed gesture of a hand stroking a cheek just means they think I'm pretty.

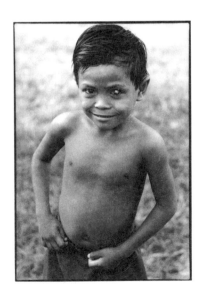

last vestiges of the "proletarian re-education" period. The prison standing next to the Governor's Palace is so dilapidated that it looks to be in ruins. Behind the gilded gate, some mad gardener seems to have reconstructed a zoo made of papier-mâché animals: A bizarre striped lion raises a paw in a silent roar; an elephant drags its soft trunk looking like it's made of plasticine; an obese and frightened deer stands wide-eyed. This odd juxtaposition adds to the naive charm that pervades the town.

Benito returns with the "taxi", an old Nissan with a rusty, dented body and broken-down seats. The road between Battambang and Sisophon is said to be one of the worst in the country. Our driver is fast and careful.

Sadly, we won't have time to enjoy his skills for very long, because after just ten kilometres something important drops off and we grind to a halt. Resigned, he flags down the first pick-up truck and tells the passengers to get out, squeezing all four of us onto a thin strip of foam that acts as the back seat. The "displaced" travellers move back to third class, standing with their bags in the back of the pick-up with everybody else. The trip is a nightmare. We are so tightly packed, on this "bone-shaker" of a back seat, that we can hardly breathe, our bags squashed under our feet or on our knees. Yet this is luxury compared to the jolts and clouds of dusts the passengers behind have to suffer. The windows are so dirty that we can't see much of the landscape outside, except for a few skeletal trees, their leaves cloaked and mummified by a coating of dried earth. It takes three hours to travel eighty kilometres. By the time we reach Sisophon it is already dark.

Sisophon

The Krousar Thmey centre in Sisophon is hidden amongst the trees on the edge of a track opposite a village. The director, a woman of around fifty, is dignified and maternal—she welcomes us warmly.

She has transformed her office into a dining room, graciously arranging the bowls and tableware, cleaned in boiled water, in the middle of the conference table. Discreet and welcoming, she offers us her dishes: strips of beef cooked in a mushroom sauce, scented rice and an overflowing plateful of "real" potato chips, cooked in palm oil. It's wonderful. Just as we're about to do honour to this meal the electricity goes off so we continue by candlelight, making us feel even more like we're in the middle of nowhere. Intrigued by the sound of children's voices repeating strangely familiar words, we follow the director to the English night class, given every other night.

Popular imagery from the times of Sangkum Reastr Niyum.

With a toothless grin, he invites us to have a go on the Roundabout, but the taxi for Sisophon is waiting for us.

More than half the children present are not at the centre but come of their own free will from nearby villages. They can register for any classes they like. When they see us, they immediately stand up and, placing their hands together, welcome us with the graceful and respectful greeting that resembles a prayer.

It's time for bed. We shower in the garden, under the full moon, hidden by a screen. I linger for a moment, bewitched by the magic of the star-filled sky and the scent of jasmine and of gardenia; I catch sight suddenly of the children unrolling their mosquito nets in the dormitories.

We're in the middle of the countryside, but the night is anything but quiet. The usual concert of dogs and cockerels interrupts our sleep, but this is nothing compared with the din coming over some loudspeakers, starting at four in the morning, when monks repeatedly chant litanies. What I took to be prayers are in fact monotonous recitations of the gifts they have received. Each morning before dawn, the monks go from house to house, carrying a bowl. Standing in rows, they wait for the occupants to serve them rice and soup. Their religion demands a vow of poverty and they must, therefore, beg

Madame Makyom has run the Sisophon centre since 1997. She's the daughter of Battambang peasants, and became a primary school teacher. When her husband died in 1973, she was left alone with 6 children. Under the Khmer rouge, she managed to hide the fact that she was an educated person, she and her children survived the camps and famine: "We lived on the roots and leaves we found near the rice fields. On three occasions, I thought we were done for... the subject is closed. "Let's us talk about he present instead..." she says.

Poipet

Monstrous trucks transport sheets of
scrap metal stacked high in piles.

The hellish border town.

The city where all sorts of trafficking happens, with a mafia that ruthlessly exploits the ever-increasing numbers of poor. Smuggling, prostitution and AIDS are rife.

to survive. The population, for their part, are duty-bound to feed them. As the monks pass, the village gradually stirs, filling with all sorts of noises: engines, shouts, hammering, as the day gets under way.

Wednesday, 5th December
Poipet

A few years ago, Poipet was just a large village. Today, it is crowded with destitute people, fleeing poverty, unemployment, debt, and family or legal problems, all seeking an improbable Eldorado. They have nothing to lose and the border town is their last hope. They try to figure out which of the countless scams rife in the town will help them to survive, or try to cross the border in the hope that prosperous neighbouring Thailand will provide them with illegal jobs. In the meantime, they are at the mercy of any number of traffickers in both the military and the mafia—whose casinos sprout overnight like malignant mushrooms, evicting and pushing families even further into slums. In barely eight years, Poipet has swollen from 20,000 to 100,000 inhabitants. Benito had warned us. This town is hardly a "pleasure trip". We try to wend our way down the middle of a wide dirty street, strewn with litter, and constantly choked with cars. Benito has to go to Thailand for supplies and leaves us on the central reservation, just in front of the border crossing. The square is filled with taxis, carts, motorcycles and scooters. The activity at the border never stops, swallowing and spitting out a tireless human mass in one direction and then in the other. We follow the movement of the crowd, constantly confronted with the cruelty and hardship of this miserable place. Here, for example, an old blind man, just skin and bones, is pulling a cart weighed down under a mountain of cardboard boxes, pushed from behind by another spectre. He is not the only one to have been transformed into a "beast of burden". We are surrounded by "slaves"

97

of all ages. Justin calls us over to show us a grown-up who's strapping layers of jeans onto a child. The scrawny youngster becomes a brawny "American footballer". Others, already padded out, wait in a row for the order to walk toward the border, like small knights in miserable armour. Children, unfortunately, are the first victims of this border hell. Abandoned or sold by families who can no longer feed them, they are traded and sent to Thailand where they beg for their 'pimps'. Picked up by the police on the pavements of Bangkok, they end up in prison and are sent back across the border—where the vicious circle starts all over again.

Krousar Thmey houses single mothers and their children in the family centre on the outskirts of Poipet. These women are the "widows", even if their husbands are still alive. It's just that they hold out little hope of seeing them again. Once their men go to Thailand to work illegally in the fields and factories, they are exploited and never manage to save enough money to come home. Desperate and humiliated, they dare not return empty-handed. The women wait in vain, some sinking into despair and even madness. There are many prostitutes in Poipet, a leading source of AIDS transmission. Some 97 percent of the prostitutes in Poipet are HIV positive.

Back to Sisophon

The Sisophon centre houses a certain number of "trafficked" children, like the one sitting in the director's arms. He's their newest arrival and he's only three, but has already been through the cycle "Poipet—Bangkok pavements—prison—return to the border" three times. Sent over in groups, the youngest children are protected under the wings of the older children, which allows the very young, from the age of two and a half, to be "trafficked". There is also an eight-year-old boy who follows us, smiling, and looking as lively and as curious as his friends. He was raped recently, several times, by an

We surprise a man piling as many layers of clothing as he can on young children, who then cross the border under the complicit eye of the custom's officers.

An indifferent Vishnu gazes down on the motorbikes, rickshaws and carts, hanging around in the dust and the rubbish, last stop before the border.

An indisputable descendant of the princes of Angkor,

Thary, the Cambodian director of Krousar Thmey.

Italian paedophile. He spoke to someone about it, and despite the tourist's denials and accusations that the boy was a liar and a thief, someone paid attention. For the moment the Italian is in jail. Trials are usually abandoned, the foreigners paying a large sum of money in exchange for their freedom. This type of exchange has also become a fairly significant source of profit for the police. From time to time, however, an NGO steps in and insists on a trial. Krousar Thmey, for example, managed to have a child smuggler they had been watching for a long time finally convicted. She received a fifteen-year sentence and has not yet been released, despite the protection she enjoys from a soldier.

Evening in Battambang

After the oppressive and difficult atmosphere of the border, Battambang seems comfortable and carefree. The blind children have prepared a surprise for us. Helped by their deaf friends, they have arranged musical instruments in one of the rooms and honour us with an improvised concert. As they play, they sit up straight and their faces light up.

Thursday, 6th December
The school run

It's five in the morning. Thary wakes Damien and myself up. The truck is leaving in fifteen minutes to pick up the schoolchildren. We move around in the dark, trying to find our bags and clothes without waking the others. We leave the centre of Battambang, crossing the river and soon finding ourselves on dirt roads. It's pitch black, but already everyone seems to be awake, and, on the path we're taking, the market is already in full swing. In fact the crowd is so thick, and the space between the stalls so small, that I wonder how we're going to make our way through in our large truck. The verges are stacked with foodstuffs. Mounds of fruit and vegetables shine in the candlelight. Displayed on round woven platters are the pieces of a freshly butchered pig, probably in preparation for a wedding. Steam rises from pots and kettles simmering over makeshift fires. It's time for soup, which serves as breakfast, lunch or dinner, and is served throughout the day. Women are crouching near the fires frying vegetables, eggs and skewers of fish, meat and poultry, but also some strange, unidentifiable creatures—rodents or reptiles maybe.

We leave the market behind. I feel like we are already very far from Battambang and yet we haven't even picked up a single student. There's no one at our first stop—no sound or movement from the house in total darkness. Finally, the driver gets out and knocks at the door. He comes back leading an adolescent holding on to his shoulder. He helps the young girl to step up over the rear of the truck. We stop repeatedly, loading a colony of children in uniform. Whenever a new deaf child jumps into the back, he doesn't sit down right away, instead he regales his friends with some amazing story, gesticulating wildly with both hands—a dangerous undertaking that seems to unbalance him at every turn, much to the hilarity of his friends. A small boy has brought a hoop and

We lean on the balcony of the terrace that overlooks the River, and watch as the day draws to a close.
An unexpected cry, just above our heads, makes us jump. "Gé-ko, gé-ko, gé-ko" screeches the gecko, its soft, reptilian body clinging to the wall.

hands it to one of the girls. Delighted, she immediately tries to use it as a hula-hoop, applauded by her over-excited friends.

It's just starting to get light. The rice paddies slowly emerge from the bluish mist, and the palm trees appear, one after another, through the dawn haze. The surface of a pond, reflecting the sky, suddenly erupts into a bright turquoise colour. A child wearing a cap fishes. Two old women, smoking, are squatting at the edge of a field and next to them the last blind student is waiting, thin as a reed. Our school truck is now full, and we return to the noisy outskirts of the town under a flamboyant fuchsia-coloured sky. The streets are packed with schoolchildren on foot, bikes and scooters. Each morning at the start of class, students and teachers raise the Cambodian flag, singing the national anthem.

Battambang wakes up under a blazing sky. Schoolchildren, workers and shopkeepers converge from all sides towards the town centre.

We got up at 5 am to follow the driver who picks the children up for school. After a two-and-a-half-hour drive, we watch the ritual that precedes each new day: the pupils stand in single file and sing the national anthem, as the flag is hoisted.

Our first trip is drawing to an end. We're flying back to Phnom Penh, in an old crate of a Soviet prop-plane!

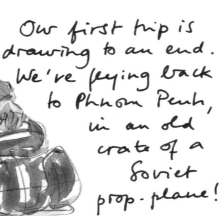

Tuol Sleng

THE SECURITY REGULATIONS
1. YOU MUST ANSWER ACCORDINGLY TO MY QUESTIONS...DON'T TURN THEM AWAY
2. DON'T TRY TO HIDE THE FACTS BY MAKING PRETEXTS THIS AND THAT. YOU ARE STRICTLY PROHIBITED TO CONTEST ME.
3. DON'T BE A FOOL FOR YOU ARE A CHAP WHO DARE TO THWART THE REVOLUTION.
4. YOU MUST IMMEDIATELY ANSWER MY QUESTIONS WITHOUT WASTING TIME TO REFLECT.
5. DON'T TELL ME EITHER ABOUT YOUR IMMORALITIES OR THE ESSENCE OF THE REVOLUTION.
6. WHILE GETTING LASHES OR ELECTRIFICATION YOU MUST NOT CRY AT ALL.
7. DO NOTHING SIT STILL AND WAIT FOR MY ORDERS. IF THERE IS NO ORDER, KEEP QUIET. WHEN I ASK YOU TO DO SOMETHING, YOU MUST DO IT RIGHT AWAY WITHOUT PROTESTING.
8. DON'T MAKE PRETEXTS ABOUT KAMPUCHEA KROM IN ORDER TO HIDE YOUR JAW OF TRAITOR.
9. IF YOU DON'T FOLLOW ALL THE ABOVE RULES, YOU SHALL GET MANY MANY LASHES OF ELECTRIC WIRE
10. IF YOU DISOBEY ANY POINT OF MY REGULATIONS YOU SHALL GET EITHER TEN LASHES OR FIVE SHOCKS OF ELECTRIC DISCHARGE.

Tuol Sleng

Constructed in the 1950s in the heart of the city, this was a high school like any other, with plain white buildings and a large courtyard planted with palm trees and fragrant frangipani. Even today, the deceptive calm and the banality of the place surprises visitors entering one of the most evil sites of the twentieth century. In 1975, the high school was taken over by the Khmer Rouge and turned into a high-security prison, known as S-21. It became the largest detention centre in the country. More than 17,000 people—men, women, children, old people and even babies—were tortured and then executed. When the Vietnamese liberated Phnom Penh, they found only seven prisoners still alive. Fourteen others had been tortured to death as their troops were moving in on the city. The soldiers buried the bodies in the courtyard and set about transforming the former high school into a museum.

We follow the signs, but hesitate before stepping into the first building, as we already feel oppressed by the place. We find rusted beds, surrounded by instruments of torture. On the wall are enlarged photos of decomposing bodies, attached to those very same beds. The main building is an incredible portrait gallery. The striking beauty, and yet the horror of the pictures, is breathtaking. Each prisoner was carefully photographed before, and sometimes after, being tortured. There are several hundred images of dazed faces staring into the camera, all looking gaunt with fear. Some pictures show the torturers, chubby-faced adolescents wearing caps.

The sheer banality and eery silence of a former school.

The barbarity of the system was such that the torturers became the tortured and were then assassinated by their replacements, all victims of successive purges within their own factions. Justin walks through the rooms looking for two faces he had seen in an English book about the restoration of Tuol Sleng. It's not easy: some of the walls are covered with photographs no larger than postage stamps. But he is determined. For him, this is like a pilgrimage, a rendez-vous with history. He has found the faces, a young boy with his prison number pinned to his bare chest and a girl, hardly ten years old. Justin then photographs them as a final tribute. In the last room, the Vietnamese have re-created a map of Cambodia using human skulls. A few tourists walk numbly through this macabre setting.

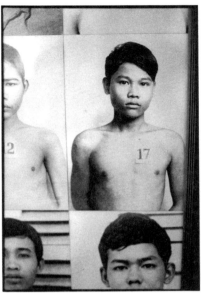

Justin has just found
the two children
he's already seen in a book.

BILAN DES PERTES CAUSEES PAR LE REGIME
GENOCIDAIRE POL POT AU KAMPUCHEA
17.4.75   7.01.79
- 3.314.768 .... TUES ET DISPARUS
- 141.868 .... INVALIDES
- 200.000 .... ORPHELINS
- 635.522 MAISONS DETRUITES PARMI LESQUELLES:
    5.857 .... ECOLES
      796 .... HOPITAUX, INFIRMERIES, LABORATOIRES
    1.968 .... PAGODES BOUDDHIQUES DETRUITES
      104 .... MOSQUEES ISLAM DETRUITS
- 1.507.416 .... BETAIL TUE
- TOUTE L'INFRASTRUCTURE INDUSTRIELLE DETRUITE DONT:
    PLUS DE 100 USINES D'ETAT ET MIXTES
    - 3.700 UNITES DE PRODUCTION ARTISANALE
- PHNOM PENH ET TOUS LES CENTRES URBAINS
(EN TOUT PLUS D'UNE CENTAINE) ABANDONNES
- TOUTE LA CAMPAGNE KAMPUCHEAENNE DONT EFFECTIVEMENT
1.200 KHUM COMPLETEMEMT EFFACEE ./.

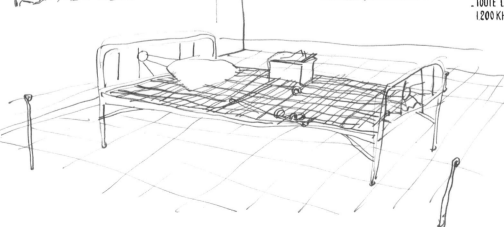

Takmau

Takmau is on the outer limits of Phnom Penh. Every Thursday afternoon, the students at the Takmau centre attend dance classes. The school is proud to have trained a talented new generation of young dancers in the last few years. The girls wear the traditional sampot, a piece of fabric looped between their legs and knotted at the waist, like baggy trousers, held in place by a finely worked silver chain. Their hair is plaited or worn in a bun, and they sit in small groups, waiting for the musicians to set up their instruments at the back of the room. Some are warming up, stretching their hands and feet—attempting to bend their fingers and feet back as far as possible. They are adorable, whispering among themselves as they glance furtively our way from time to time. The boys test their strings and cymbals, and then sitting down; with bows and sticks raised, begin to practise the scales. Someone brings us chairs and large coconuts with straws to refresh us. The dancers are aged between five and fifteen years. The oldest girls start first, under the strict supervision of their professor. Serious and concentrated, they perform a few movements, following one another in a sinuous co-ordinated line. The boys then join in for the traditional dances that mime the essential stages of rice planting and harvesting. As accessories, they hold branches and scythes. Their faces light up, and the dancing becomes more and more joyful and frenetic. Delighted, we give them a standing ovation. Then we pose with them for the classic souvenir photo, which may join the patchwork of pictures pinned on the wall. They proudly show us a photograph of the queen, present at the opening ceremony, next to another of "Gérard and Carole", stars of French cinema, who visited the school last autumn.

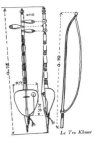

the gong announces the beginning of the rehearsal.
the little girls spread out, like a living frieze,
their backs and fingers arched, toes pointed
and muscular thighs tensed with the effort.

The boys carry the instruments to the rehearsal room.

Damien spares a thought for Josephine, his 9 years old daughter whom he often takes to dancing classes. He can see the same concentration, Rigour and grace in the gestures of the little Cambodian girls.

របាំគោះក្រទ្លោក

Coconut Dance

Phnom Penh

Stop over in Bangkok.

Friday, 15th February 2002

It's been barely two months since our last trip. Phnom Penh looks as if we had just left the day before; we're happy to be back and everything looks familiar. It's definitely hotter this time, but nothing compared to the burning heat of April and May, which lasts until the rains finally arrive in June. The entire population, exhausted and parched by then, awaits this "liberation by rain" with growing impatience, disappointed and irritated when the sky plays tricks, with threatening storm clouds, which refuse to burst for up to a week. As if to mock the dry, yellowed grass verges and omnipresent grey dust the trees in Phnom Penh—yellow mimosa, mauve-violet jacaranda, fuchsia-coloured bougainvillaea, acacia, pinkish-ivory and bright orange frangipani—are in full bloom. We pull up in front of the green entrance gate, decorated with the large Krousar Thmey butterfly with a group of children under the protection of its outstretched wings. The door opens even before Benito has a chance to honk, and we are greeted by the radiant smiles and welcoming cries of the entire small community that lives and works at "La Casa".

A pile of newspapers sits on a table: issues of the *Cambodian Daily*, *Cambodge Soir* and the *Phnom Penh Post* from the past ten days. They are filled with the results and analysis of the February municipal elections. Indeed, we had seen many campaign posters along the roads in December. The election results surprised everyone, both the local population and the foreign observers. Many people thought the opposition parties, such as the PSR (Sam Rainsy's party, the leading opponent to Prime Minister Hun Sen) and the FUNCINPEC (the party of King Sihanouk's son, Prince Ranariddh) would gain ground. In the end, the PCC retained a large majority, with 61 percent, of the vote. Some newspapers reported strong-arm tactics in towns where the opposition could have won a majority. Yet with "only" fifteen deaths, everyone seems to agree that the elections took place in relative calm and produced satisfactory results. The European Union did mention that these elections were neither fair nor open—a reasonably predictable comment for a country where the one-person, one-vote system was only reinstated in 1993.

FCC

Phnom Penh Post

The Wat Botthom, a pagoda with a community of 247 monks.

We meet Benito in the hushed atmosphere of a former colonial club, the FCC (Foreign Correspondents' Club) where he comments on the latest election Results.

MINISTRY OF INDUSTRY AND ENERGY

In front of the ministry of Industry and Energy.

A fan for a halo!

Bertrand Porte's office.

Heads, statues and pieces of stone waiting to be restored among jars of pigments and resins.

The National Museum restoration workshop

During our last trip we were not able to meet Bertrand Porte, director of the National Museum's restoration workshop, so we head straight back to find him as soon as we arrive. It's mid-afternoon when we enter the first room of the workshop.

The main room contains unusual and unique works that are awaiting analysis and restoration. Bertrand Porte shows us a few pieces that are in the process of being restored, for example, a seventh-century Durga[29] that was recently discovered near Kompong Speu by farmers digging in a field. They found all the pieces, the beautiful head, the body and the four arms, separately. She is holding a dagger-sized sword in one hand, while the fingers of another hand are joined to form a circle, into which bronze artefacts were placed. Next to this sculpture is a small pre-Angkor Buddha waiting a cleaning process that will remove the ornamentation that was added later to "update" it. Restoration is a delicate process. The layers of paint are scraped off and the different pieces are separated to remove the cement joints; these pieces are then put back together using ancient techniques. This process will be used for the large Devatas standing against the wall. The previous restoration was poorly done: cracks in the stone were concealed with cement or resin, and sometimes entirely covered and polished to make the works look smooth and new. Bertrand Porte recently submitted a request to France, after he realised that he had managed, over the years, to find the various elements of a major work. The head, however, is in the Guimet Museum in Paris. He would like to re-create the entire statue and return it to Phnom Penh. He is trying to negotiate an exchange with the French museum. Another lucky discovery by monks was that of a horse's head; Porte has found the original setting of the work in a temple, on the body of a Man-God—no one had ever imagined that it included a horse's head.

Bertrand Porte has run the restoration workshop since 1997.

He is surrounded by five Cambodian apprentices, Art school students or autodidacts, like the former museum warden, who was so gifted that he was employed without any diploma.

Created and opened by Roland Coignard[30] in 1995, the workshop survives thanks to a budget which Bertrand Porte, who took over in 1997, has to renegotiate every year with the French Culture Ministry. He also receives some private funding and help from the École Française d'Extrême-Orient. Appointed for three years, he is about to renew his contract for the third time. I ask him why he decided to move to Cambodia; smiling, he replies "By pure chance!" He had recently graduated and was working on the restoration of Notre-Dame in Paris. He had absolutely no knowledge of Asian art, but one day he learned that a position had opened up in Phnom Penh, so he submitted an application, without really expecting anything to come of it. So it was a huge surprise when he learned that he had been selected. He raced over to the Guimet Museum to learn what he could before leaving, but sadly this was closed for restoration. He therefore left as a neophyte, to a country that immediately adopted and charmed him. And he hasn't thought about leaving since, especially as he is deeply involved in a new project to restore the collections in regional areas and in Vietnam, in close collaboration with the Cernushi and Guimet Museums.

Although few drivers wear them,
a whole street displays brand new helmets for sale.

We notice new shops that provide telephone services
via the Internet, a very recent "enterprise"
which is not yet regulated.

នៅពេលអ្នកទិញស្រោមអនាម័យក្រោយទៀត ដើម្បី
ជាការដាយស្រួល អ្នកអាចបំពេញឈ្មោះបណ្ណខាង
ក្រោម ដោយគ្រាន់តែគូសយកម្ដាក់ចំនួនកញ្ចប់ណាមួយ
ដែលអ្នកចង់បាន ហើយប្រគល់ឲ្យអ្នកលក់ ។
លោក លោកស្រី ជានីគោរព
ខ្ញុំត្រូវការ ចាб: ចំនួនប្រអប់

NUMBER ONE កញ្ចប់ស្រោមб ☐

NUMBER ONE
Quality Condoms from PSI

Around the Independance
Monument. At night it
shines like a lighthouse,
with the colours of the
Cambodian flag:
blue, red, blue.

Tuesday, 16th February, Catherine Théron

I wanted to visit Catherine Théron, about whom I'd heard in France. There was a magnificent exhibition at UNESCO of silks she had designed and had had woven by Cambodian weavers. Benito knows her, and admires her work and the perseverance with which she manages to run, single-handedly, her small company.

Catherine lives on a peaceful street in the centre of Phnom Penh, behind the Wat Botthom. On the first floor of a little white house she has made a cosy and intimate home: silk shawls are suspended like paintings on the walls, along with a some framed black and white photographs of Angkor and a few lovely objects, reminders of her travels. Catherine tells us her story, which actually starts with that of her father. Jacques Théron was born in Hanoi, where he spent his childhood. In the late 1950s, he was appointed director of two rubber plantations that belonged to the French company Les Plantations Réunies de Mimot in the Kompong Cham region. He spent fifteen years in Cambodia, until the start of the civil war in 1971, when he was repatriated. He was  then sent on new assignments, to sugar palm plantations in Indonesia, Sumatra and Djakarta. His last job took him back to the country of his youth, Vietnam. During this mission, he managed to enter Cambodia in 1989, after eighteen years. He went to his former plantation, where the rare survivors from the Khmer Rouge period greeted him like a father. Of the 4,000 workers and 40 managers who worked on the two plantations, those remaining could be counted on the fingers of one hand. Catherine went along with him on a second, very brief, trip five years later, in 1994. Returning to the land of her childhood had a profound effect. At the time Phnom Penh was still an extremely militarised zone. Catherine talks about the "indescribable shock" she felt. The plant-

ations were under heavy surveillance. The rubber was sent illegally to Vietnam, there were all kinds of smuggling activities. As if it were yesterday she remembers the row of heavily armed guards that pointed their AK-47s straight at them as they got out of their car. She had already noticed the large number of vehicles escorted by motorcycles, transporting soldiers armed with machine guns and rocket launchers. In 1994, with warring factions everywhere, kidnapping was common place and no important figure went out without bodyguards. At the plantation, the former foreman and the few survivors started crying as they drove up. An old woman, who Jacques Théron didn't recognise at first, stood hunched up in front of them. He then realised that she was the young girl who used to look after his children. Scarred by years of war, terror and famine, she was unrecognisable.

Catherine then decided to live in Asia. She tried to promote Khmer crafts by creating designs and having them made by women living in regions that still use traditional techniques for dyeing and weaving. She faced many problems. Silk manufacture is a local, handmade craft in Cambodia. It is therefore expensive, as opposed to silk from India or Thailand, where intensive production techniques produce textiles at unbeatable prices. Also an entire new generation of women had to be trained, as many of the techniques of their elders had been lost. And the weavers are very good at reproducing traditional designs, but as soon as Catherine asks them for a bit of creativity they resist. It's hard for them to adapt and they have to be walked through the process, step by step. Yet the growing Western demand for silk means that the old designs have to be updated. Two years ago she created her own label, Kashaya. We leave with regret, marvelling at her scarves and entranced by her charming personality.

In 1971, Catherine was only four years old when her father, who was manager of a rubber plantation, left Cambodia.

Jacques Thiron

She led a nomadic life in Indonesia, then in South Africa and Thailand. An irresistible attraction drew her back to the country of her early childhood, where she settled in 1994, devoting herself to the creation of textiles.

Wat Botthom

We walk around the elegant pagoda as we leave Catherine's, and we finally decide to go inside, intrigued by the voices and laughter ringing out from behind a forest of stupas. We discover the existence of a village of monks, a community of 750 people, including 247 monks and three elderly nuns, who do the cooking. Their bright orange and yellow robes are drying on lines. A group of them are playing volleyball. The others are praying on the terraces or watching us with curiosity. Breaking the overall calm of the place, a young monk, mobile phone to his ear, walks back and forth, in the midst of a loud and lively conversation. Our three guides are between twenty-two and twenty-five years old and entered the community when they were four, five and seven, respectively. They all come from provincial areas, but none of them wishes to remain a monk. They, like everyone else, want to earn "dollars".

I had imagined the "master" to be a venerable monk, getting on in years, but this one is only 30, looks like an American actor, and is disconcertingly mischievous.

His back is tattooed all over with Buddhist texts.

VEN. MORN CHHAIYUTD of Cambodian
 វិនៈ ម៉ន ឆៃយុទ្ធ

30

The monks' robes dry between the stupas. Justin has found the remains of a card game on the ground.

119

THE MEKONG

The cigar-shaped "Jet-boats" that sail up the Mekong and the Tonle Sap.

Passagers and porters jostle each other on the roof of the boat to get a good place for the trip. Soon there's no room left. We're surrounded by families, and by tradeswomen who are going back to their villages, having stocked up with supplies in Phnom Penh.

A young man manages to get a scooter on board, acrobatically lifting it all the way along the boat's narrow edge.

Sunday, 17th February
Sailing up the Mekong

The river port is upstream from the floating "Naga Casino", an enormous ship that looks like a huge beached toad. Departure time is at 7am, aboard one of the fast cigar-shaped boats. We are among the first to climb aboard the white hull and sit with our feet propped up against the guard-rail. We have to squeeze closer together as more and more passengers arrive. The boats on the Mekong have fewer tourists than those going up the Tonle Sap River to Siem Reap and those with us today are young backpackers. This is the Cambodians' favourite means of travel, but only the relatively well-off, mostly traders, can afford to take them. The trip is expensive, but it's faster and more comfortable than by car. There is little choice as, with the exception of two derelict lines linking Phnom Penh to the north and to the south-west, at speeds of about 20 kph, there are no trains and few people have their own cars. Communal "pick-up" trucks are therefore the normal means to get around.

The source of the Mekong is in Tibet. The river crosses China, Burma, Laos and 486 kilometres of Cambodia, before flowing into the China Sea from South Vietnam. Five kilometres wide in places, the river floods often, leaving rich sediment and extremely fertile mud along the banks. It is navigable upstream from September to February, when the water level is high. For this first stage, we plan to stop in Kratie and from there we hope to be able to get to Stung Treng, near the Laotian border. We make a first stop at one of the picturesque villages, although the riverbanks are used as public rubbish dumps. A young woman, accompanied by her sister, mother and aunt, lifts her basket onto her head, takes her young boy by the hand and climbs up the roughly formed steps in the mud bank—wearing high-heeled sandals. I am often surprised to see such urban, and seemingly unsuitable, clothing worn by fashionable young Cambodians. At each stop, a swarm of vendors comes on board. They weave among the passengers, proposing their wares: bunches of passion fruit in pinkish-beige shells; strange sticks of sugar cane that peel like bananas on a tube of compressed sticky rice; or small packages wrapped in leaves. What a disappointment these are! Inside is a second, then a third layer of wrapping, with nothing but a small, inedible and spicy lozenge in the middle. A few monks come aboard and sit in the back, rolling and unrolling their long orange robes. The unrelenting heat overwhelms us each time we stop. Benito shakes me awake so that I don't miss the sight of the immense bridge at Kompong Cham, which was inaugurated last December. This thriving city will soon threaten Battambang as Cambodia's second largest city, after Phnom Penh. The bridge has become the region's most popular attraction and is always swarming with visitors. It's 1pm when we reach the steep riverbank at Kratie. It's burning hot, despite the temporary shade provided by the large eucalyptus leaves, which flutter with the slightest breeze. Rebuffing the offers of "helpful" advice, we follow the young man we met on the boat. Now that we're on solid ground, we discover that he is club-footed, his legs are spindly and deformed.

Kratie can be described succinctly: a dock, a main street, three blocks of houses, a market and a single tourist attraction—the last freshwater dolphins in the Mekong.

This alone justifies the existence of a few rundown hotels and a small armada of motodops. We visit three guesthouses and choose the one that looks the cleanest and quietest, with the additional bonus of a river view. The Heng-Heng Hotel is run by a Chinese family, as are almost all of the businesses in town. A sign at the entrance sets out the rules, which Justin copies, word for word, in his notebook. Rule n°.3: It is forbidden to bring into the hotel any category of explosives or other inflammable substances, drugs or poisons. Rule n°.4: All forms of prostitution and gambling are strictly forbidden.

We have just to cross the street for lunch at the Mekong, run by a very stout Sino-Khmer; it seems clear that his influence in this small local community extends far beyond this restaurant. He greets us warmly and with a great deal of attention, assisted by an entire group of female figures ranging from four to sixty years of age: they are all part of his family. Discreet and cheerful, they serve us copious portions of food: a "pot-au-feu" with fish and mushrooms, beef with green peppers, pork with fried noodles and rice. As an after-meal "digestif" drink, they propose the bright orange concoction that Benito adores, cold lemon tea with cochineal. A mob of motodops has gathered on the pavement while we've been eating lunch. They are waiting to take us to the site, some fifteen kilometres from the city, where we can see the Irrawaddy dolphins. There may be no more than sixty of them left, all

គោជ័យដ្ឋាន មេកុង
MEKONG RESTAURANT
ខ្មុមខេត្តក្រចេះ
KRATIE PROVINCE

HENG HENG HOTEL

Soap

Kratie Province
Tel : 072-971 405

Mr. "Mekong", the Chinese owner of the best restaurant in Kratie.

Kieng Thy

Kratie: all the charm of a small provincial town.

An adorable little girl swings in a hammock over a mountain of scooped-out coconuts and sugar-cane peelings, which her mother puts in a press. One young man splits open the coconuts, and another serves the juice.

The strange monument dedicated to the "Irrawaddy" the last fresh water dolphins.

in this part of the Mekong, north of Kratie. We choose four motodops among the dozen or so that rush up to us as we leave the restaurant. We take a pretty countryside road along the river. The land is unrecognisable from our last trip. In barely two months, the lush, green, water-soaked rice paddies have become khaki-coloured, dried-up fields. The houses on stilts are as pretty as ever, but they seem to be isolated and less cheerful without their ponds—now scorched and grey.

The observation deck is characterised by a life-size painted statue of a dolphin upon a cement base. It's the perfect subject for Damien, who loves any architecture, statue or panels reminiscent of the 1950s. We meet the disabled young man from the boat at the Dolphin Lodge, and we realise that he's the leader of a group, directing all the others and running the tourist business. Two boats are tied up in the creek. The price proposed, three dollars per person, seems too high, so we decide to wait. And, in fact, it's still too hot to go out on the water. We sit quietly in the shade of the acacia trees. Tourists come along and climb aboard the boats. We have no regrets as they leave, especially as Justin and Benito have just spotted a group of dolphins, leaping and diving, not far from our perch near the riverbank. A Swiss man we noticed on the ferry this morning pulls on pink flippers and swims towards them. The backs of the dolphins shimmer in the soft, silver, late-afternoon light. We are almost alone now; the tourists are a long way off, in the middle of the river not realising the dolphins are far away.

On the road back, my motodop almost hits a pig, a bicycle, a chicken and its chicks, not to mention an entire herd of water buffalo and their offspring.

We have a drink on the quayside, where women have set up trestle tables covered with gaudy lino tablecloths. We sit on the plastic chairs, dog-tired, but in awe of a magnificent pink sunset reflected in successive ripples of colour on the river.

We can't walk anywhere with Benito without him immediately recognising someone, even here in Kratie, which he is visiting for the first time. Vanna, interrupted in mid-evening jog, hugs him. He is a former Cambodian refugee who was able to obtain a visa for France in 1979. He's forty-two. After spending a few years with a foster family, he decided to return to his homeland in 1994, with the goal of creating a company and, above all, to fulfil his dream: to help the reconstruction of his ravaged country, deprived of so many trained and competent Cambodians. He joins us for dinner at the Mekong Restaurant, which has become our head-quarters. We are so happy to be with a Cambodian who speaks French that we bombard him with questions. He seems to be pleased by our interest, and tells us his life story. He was fourteen in 1975. Evicted by brigades of Khmer Rouge, he took to the roads with thousands of other city-dwellers and was separated from his family—each person was sent to a different camp. He had to work very hard in the rice paddies. Their guards terrorised and starved them, so he, along with two friends, tried to kill a cow. This was discovered and the young boys were denounced during the sessions of self-criticism.

Vanna managed to remain alive thanks to the protection of one of the guards, who came from his village, but he was then sent to an even tougher camp on the Vietnamese border. There he witnessed the daily executions. Once again, his only chance of survival was to steal. One day he decided to escape and managed to cross the border, where he was captured by Vietnamese soldiers who sent him, with some forty other Cambodian refugees, to a prison. He was the youngest, but he quickly learned Vietnamese and became an interpreter for the group, shuttling back and forth from the prison to the courts. During all these months, he was constantly putting together escape plans with his friends, trying to find ways to get to Thailand along the coast. These were finally abandoned, being far too dangerous and simply not feasible. He then began to think about a wild idea: to travel to Thailand via the north, crossing Cambodia. It took him and his two friends four terrifying months; they moved cautiously through the forest, remaining hidden most of the time. Racked by hunger and fear, they were nearly discovered several times. Finally, however, they managed to cross the border. Once there, they took off their clothes to wave them like white flags. He laughs now thinking about it, as the uniform imposed by the Khmer Rouge consisted of a black shirt and trousers. They were imprisoned, then placed in a refugee camp. They were lucky, avoiding the special brigades that came looking for escaped prisoners in the camps to take them by bus, not to Bangkok, but to unload them at the border, in the forests bristling with land mines. Hundreds of traumatised and terrorised victims found themselves like this, trapped between gunfire from the Thai soldiers forcing them forward and shots from the Khmer Rouge who were waiting to pick them off like rabbits. It was a hellish nightmare; exhausted, panicked and desperate, thousands suffered and then perished in the mud.

Back at the hotel, I notice a group of strong-looking young American soldiers, finishing their dinner. Curious, we ask the restaurant owner and find out that they are part of an "M.I.A." (Missing in Action) group. They are trying to find the bodies of soldiers who fought in Vietnam and Cambodia. Years have gone by, but time has not yet healed the wounds. And for all families—Vietnamese, Cambodian or American—one identified bone, no matter how small or insignificant, can help in the process of grieving for a lost relative.

Vanna is a former Cambodian refugee who fled to France. He tells us the story of what he endured under the Khmer rouge and about his fight for survival. Despite the indelible trauma, he wanted to return and help the reconstruction of his country.

KAO Vannarin
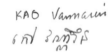

The young woman serves us warm beer and prepares the crockery and ingredients for the soup. Plucked chicken heads, still sporting their combs, dangle from a basin.

At the Kratie market, the fishmongers squat on large wooden platforms.

The gestures are quick and precise: grabbing, weighing, cutting, then holding the quivering pieces.

The fruit and vegetable sellers.

The poultry seller
who insisted I sketch her.

She sits up straight,
proud to be the
center of attention.
Her neighbours
tease her and
make comments.

129

Monday, 18th February
A day in Kratie

Benito had wanted to take a boat today to travel up the Mekong to Stung Treng, a trip renowned for it's wild beauty. But the boat only runs every two days. We are happy to have a day off, allowing us to discover Kratie, whose atmosphere and remoteness have charmed us. Drawn to the main market like a magnet, we plunge into the heart of it, following the narrow alleys that criss-cross the interior. Women are crouched on tables as large as platforms. I stop at a fish stand, fascinated by some enormous tubs filled with live eels. I shudder as I watch the shimmering undulating creatures being cut up—they have to be skinned alive otherwise the flavour changes. Word has travelled around the market that I'm drawing, and a crowd gathers around me. As soon as I finish my first sketch, a women pulls me by the arm to her chicken stand, so that I can draw her. Hundreds of chickens, tied-up, are clucking under the platform. Others have been plucked and placed, feet in the air, in pails. Further on, very young girls disappear behind pyramids of cabbages,

white-root vegetables, carrots, tomatoes, courgettes and onions, selling a handful here and there—in such small quantities that I wonder how they manage to sell all their goods.

It's noon. The heat is unbearable; indeed, the town has emptied for a few hours. There's nothing else to do but take a nap. We seek refuge at Mr. "Mekong's" and Benito tells him I'd like to draw his portrait. When I finish, he signs his name twice, once in Chinese and once in Cambodian. He is Sino-Khmer, like most of the merchants who immigrated to Cambodia, and has married a local woman. The Chinese play a considerable role in the country. They are both shop-owners and traders, and a large portion of the Cambodian population depends on their services. They sell imported items on credit, especially to farmers, and they receive payment in the form of produce, which they then export. It's a low-cost business that contributes to the economy of rural life. As moneylenders, however, they charge an exorbitant interest rate of 100 percent over nine months, which means that many farmers are deep in debt. The government has tried, unsuccessfully, to replace the "Chinese lenders". Co-operatives and other government-owned stores have been even more inefficient, thanks to the dishonesty of the middlemen.

The Heng-Heng is full so we have to change hotels. As we gather up our bags, the owner sits down on the pavement and starts picking lice from the heads of each of her grandchildren, who stand patiently in line, waiting their turn and scratching their heads. We look at three guesthouses, each one more sordid than the last, and we finally opt for the third one. Despite the red nylon sheets, it has, at least, rooms with windows and a balcony. We go to the market to buy a few metres of krama to replace the nylon sheets. We immediately soak and wash them to remove the starch. This operation is soon abandoned. Not only is the drain blocked but Justin and Benito run out, horrified, as excrement is floating to the top in the nearby bathrooms and the stench is unbearable. Laughing hysterically, we call a maid, who fetches the owner. He tries to unblock the pipes but this only makes matters worse, and the smell is now filling our room, while the bathroom floor is flooding with a brackish liquid. In a flash, we return to the second guesthouse, the one without windows, but at least it has fairly clean sheets.

We are interrupted by a man on a motodop who has bad news: there is no boat tomorrow. The one we were supposed to take ran aground on a sandbank today, on

This other vegetable seller, who poses for Damien, does her best not to laugh, not wanting to show her bad teeth.

At all times of the day men, women and children come here to drink soup.

SEANG BISEY
ស៊ាង - ប៊ីស៊ី
I am Twenty-five
years old!
25 ans

In this hairdresser's salon that opens onto the street, a young girl is having her hair and make-up done for a wedding. Dresses fit for a Princess

have been rented for the occasion, and are hanging in a Formica wardrobe. Each is more kitsch than the next, with nylon, lace, sequins and frills.

The beauty's fiancé arrives a little impatient. But he's not surprised to see his girlfriend's naturally pretty face transformed into a stiff, garish mask.

The beauty treatment for men is more basic.

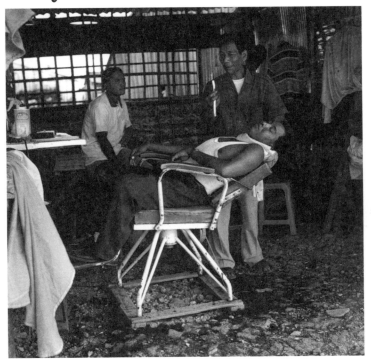

the way back from Stung Treng, and the hull is cracked. It's the end of the season, the level of the river has dropped and the trip has become too dangerous. We are very disappointed, especially as many people had told us how beautiful the trip is. Benito leaves immediately to find a taxi for tomorrow.

We have one last dinner at the Mekong, where the owner spoils us and produces delicious fried potatoes. The electricity goes off twice during the evening. He hooks up the generator and flips the television to CNN: there's been another attack in Israel; this report is followed by images of Baghdad and Afghanistan. Another channel broadcasts footage of policemen chasing and beating demonstrators in the corridors of a building in South Korea. Benito tells us that all of King Sihanouk's bodyguards are North Korean, having a reputation for speed and efficiency. We switch channels again and see Hun Sen amongst a group of women, discussing parliamentary projects. His wife is heavily involved in politics. After this is a sequence on a front porch somewhere, where the prime minister's henchmen display the gifts that he will give to the poor, explaining what they are, just like some TV shopping channel.

Damien and his faithful side-kick.

Tuesday, 19th February
On the road to Ratanakiri

Before starting out for Ban Lung, the capital of Ratanakiri province near the Vietnamese border, we exchange some dollars for riels with one of the jewellers standing behind his glass-fronted trolley parked on the pavement. Benito arrives with the taxi. He thinks it should take from five to eight hours to drive the 300 kilometres. The countryside is beautiful, still lush and green, as we drive alongside the Mekong. We glimpse the small wooded islands that emerge from the river at this time of year, as the water levels drop. The riverbanks are bursting with life. The minute we turn off to the east, however, and move away from the Mekong, the landscape suddenly transforms itself into something like the African bush; scorched yellow and very dry, with stunted trees and termite mounds. We don't see any people, animals or homes. Life seems to have disappeared from this inhospitable region. It looks as if fires have ravaged the woods through which we're driving. The origins of these fires are neither accidental nor criminal. Benito explains that, in order to pay to have the roads repaired, the government allows the companies to exploit all the wood along a fifty-metre strip adjoining the road.

The road turns into a dusty red dirt track and starts to rise imperceptibly toward the high plateaux of Ratanakiri.

Ban Lung, a setting worthy of a western.

Halfway, we stop for lunch in a cheap restaurant whose only room serves as dining room, grocer's shop and the family accommodation.

The walls are covered in adverts for shampoos, canned drinks and beers.

The rubber plantations.

As we climb in altitude, the landscape becomes greener and there are more valleys. There are also fields of shiny-leafed shrubs; the hard shells on the branches contain cashew nuts. A dense, primeval forest is gaining ground here. Shortly before we arrive at Ban Lung, rubber plantations gradually take over. Their immense majestic trees, with light-coloured trunks, are each scarred with a single, long spiralling line, from which flows the sticky white sap that is collected in earthenware containers.

It's 3:15pm when we reach Ban Lung, after a six-hour drive. The wide road leading to the town's central round-about is empty. The wind is blowing, raising swirls of red dust. The only recommended hotel, the "Terre Rouge", is full. The best rooms at the Mountain Guesthouse are already taken and the others are gloomy. Someone suggests the Mountain Guesthouse II. It's just a hundred metres away, off the main street, and we like it immediately. It's not in great shape anymore, but this former home still has a colonial charm, with a volleyball net strung up between the mango trees in the garden. Men are working on scaffolding that covers the main entrance. They are all Vietnamese, as is almost all of the local labour—men who have crossed the border to settle in the region. Justin is charmed. He loves this doddering old building, with Art Deco tiles on the floor and a spacious terrace, with no scaffolding to spoil the view. There is another advantage: it's clean and quiet, and it looks as though we're the only occupants in this intriguing "ghosthouse". It's five o'clock, the workers have finished their day and we enjoy the welcome serenity of late afternoon, comfortably installed in armchairs on the terrace, all of us writing in our notebooks. It's time for the daily volleyball match between the workers and the hotel staff. After the game, two of them try to knock down some mangoes, using a long stick; they take aim carefully and hit the fruit hidden in the lush shiny leaves. Like incense, the smell of burning grass rises gently from a fire nearby.

Wednesday, 20th February
Ban Lung market

We want to arrive early at the market, where women from the primitive Kreung[31] tribes come every day. These are ethnic minorities that live in the wooded highlands that straddle Cambodia, Laos and Vietnam. They walk many kilometres each day carrying fruit and vegetables in woven baskets strapped to their backs. Seated on the ground all around the covered market, they are easily distinguished from Cambodian women: being smaller and more muscular with delicate and pronounced features. They are similar in morphology to Thais or to the

Near the lake, a portrait of a very young King Sihanouk.

In front of our guesthouse, where building work is being done, the workmen play volleyball with the caretakers.

In our travels, we encounter strange, painted concrete animals creating a comical and grotesque bestiary in the landscape.

អដ្ឋិកូរណា

The improbable entrance to a former barracks.

Ban Lung market.

Aerosol sprays to refill lighters.

The women of the Kreung tribes, ethnic minorities that straddle the borders of Cambodia, Laos and Viêt Nam.

The roof of the covered market.

They walk for hours everyday, between their distant villages and the market, carrying various vegetables and fruits.

Burmese. I sit down in their midst to draw. This is the first time I sense some reticence, a quiet irritation and even hostility directed towards me. Yet my presence attracts the usual curiosity, and I hear laughter all around. Justin also feels ill at east. Neither of us means to treat these dreadfully poor women like animals in a zoo so, for the first time, we slip them a little money as thanks for posing for us, especially as the chaos we've caused certainly prevented them from selling their produce.

A wedding

Benito calls to us. He has spotted a wedding ceremony in a nearby street. We hurry over and follow him to a tent where the entrance is decorated with fluorescent-coloured curtains, palm branches, Chinese lanterns, and bunches of bananas and coconuts spray-painted gold. The ceremony starts with a procession early in the morning. Monks, the master of ceremonies and guests accompany the groom and his family as far as the house of his future bride's parents to present offerings. There, the groom introduces himself and asks his prospective father-in-law if he is satisfied with the gifts and if he agrees to give his daughter's hand in marriage. The father then invites his future son-in-law and guests to sit down in chairs arranged in rows facing each other. The bride appears and walks on a red carpet toward her fiancé. Then a number of rituals are performed with an introductory speech and blessings for the couple, and for the families, before the meal. We arrive right in the middle of all this. The bride and groom are standing with their heads lowered, holding hands and looking serious and concentrated. Their chairs are gilded and covered with fake red fur to set them off from the others and make them look like thrones. They are surrounded by their witnesses and their attendants: two young girls wearing Barbie-pink dresses and two young men in white Prince Charming outfits, with gilt buttons and silk scarves.

139

A wedding ceremony begins at dawn, when relatives, carrying offerings, escort the bridegroom as far as the bride's parent's home.

Most marriages are still arranged by families from the same background. The main offerings are displayed on platters on a table at the entrance: an enormous pig's head with all the entrails, fruit, flowers, cigarettes, jewels and other small wrapped objects complete the collection of gifts to the "spirits". My reverie is interrupted by the appearance of a clown with red circles on his forehead and cheeks and a black moustache painted under his nose. He is the spitting image of Charlie Chaplin and has been hired to keep the atmosphere lively. Highly sprung, like some clockwork toy, he teases and provokes the poor attendants, much to the hilarity of the guests. He walks around them, coaxing and challenging them to laugh, especially the girls, but can't even raise a smile. In fact, they become even more serious and try to ignore him. The joker plays with a mirror; on the reverse side is a picture of a pin-up. He pulls out a wedding ring that he slips through the couple's hair and cuts a small lock from each. Then he repeats the same schoolboy jokes, working the crowd up. We politely decline the father's invitation to stay for lunch. The guests participate in the dowry by slipping a few banknotes into a box before the meal. It also helps defray some of the expenses. A good wedding can cost up to a thousand dollars.

The Kreung tribes

We leave Ban Lung, looking for one of the villages at the edge of the forest, home to the Kreung tribes. We pass a group of women returning from market, their baskets empty. We take potluck, choosing one of the tracks off the main road, and are soon stopped short by a rope strung across our path—is it protecting or restricting the entrance to the village? We park our scooters, hurdle the rope and are greeted by a group of women, children and old men. All are thin and miserable looking, their skin is dry and gnarled like old grapevines. The women are bare-breasted and smoke pipes that they stick occasionally in their hair, like combs. Benito and Justin follow two tipsy adults and are surprised to

"There is no waste in a pig." The traditional dish

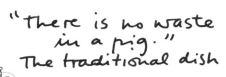

at Cambodian weddings proves just that!

After the religious ritual, a clown arrives to warm up the audience.

discover that one of the huts is full of a dozen men, all wildly drunk, smoking and drinking palm wine. February is a quiet month for these peasants, so they use the time to relax. Benito is saddened both by the decrepit state of the village and by the lack of hygiene. I sit down in the shade of a mango tree to draw the small group that greeted us, in front of one of the huts whose woven bamboo walls are decorated with geometric patterns. Again we leave a little money with one of the "elders", as agreed upon by Benito, in exchange for letting us enter their village.

Terre Rouge

We dine at "Terre Rouge", a lodge opened a year ago in Ban Lung by a young Frenchman, Pierre-Yves, and his Cambodian wife, Chenda. Pierre-Yves works as a guide for tourist groups that he escorts throughout the country, while Chenda manages the hotel, assisted by her mother and her many aunts, nieces and cousins. As is the custom in Cambodia every new bride gathers her family around her, especially if she has improved her social status. Happy and proud, they show us their five-month-old son. Pierre-Yves tells us about his day: he took his group to visit some of the most primitive and beautiful villages, then taking them on an elephant ride. He would like to buy two or three for "Terre Rouge" but, even without including the wages for the elephant-keeper and all the necessary upkeep, the price is too high at 20,000 dollars per animal. He's sorry that we're leaving tomorrow and insists on a volunteer: he promises to send a guide to take one of us to photograph, or draw, the most beautiful bachelor's hut in the region. It's at least an hour away, and the plane is at 11am; it's possible. Of course I am chosen: I'll be the emissary of the "Trois Moustiquaires", sent to immortalise a small shack on giant stilts. This is where every young man over seventeen is sequestered until his marriage, to prevent any stray "hormonal impulses" that may cause trouble.

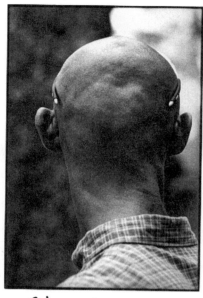

Pierre-Yves, "Close encounters of the third kind".

Chenda, his Cambodian wife, runs the "Terre Rouge" hotel while he takes his groups all over the country

142

The village is deserted, except for a few old men who are looking after a horde of timid, sickly children.

On the last day, a guide of "Terre Rouge" fetches me at dawn to take me to a distant village where the tallest bachelor hut is to be found.

Pierre-Yves has set up a table for us in the garden, where an American is already seated. Jeff Rock lives in Bangkok, where he works for the State Department. We ask him what he's doing in Ban Lung, but he remains evasive. A Mormon and father of three adult children, he's a strong believer in the role of missionaries in the third world. Benito provokes him a little, but our man doesn't seem to appreciate the humour. The conversation moves on to less sensitive subjects. He was in Phnom Penh during the brief attempted coup d'etat in 1997. He still regrets that the American authorities panicked and ordered him to evacuate immediately, when it wasn't necessary. He was extremely angry that his superiors didn't listen to the opinions of their representatives on the ground. Jeff Rock slips away quietly, on the pretext of picking up an e-mail from Washington. Benito watches, smiling slyly: "Guess who else is in Ban Lung right now? Sam Rainsy, the main leader of the Cambodian opposition."

Thursday, 21st February
The remote village

It's seven in the morning. The young guide from "Terre Rouge" is on time. We don't have a minute to lose; I slip on a long-sleeved shirt to protect me from the sun and tie a krama under my hat. Damien seems anxious that I'm leaving on my own. What if I miss the plane? I decide not to think about it and off we go, following a winding road. The trip is magnificent; we go further and further into the virgin forests, dominated by enormous liana-covered trees. The vegetation is thick, damp and dark. Tufts of wild orchids grow on the tree trunks and hang from branches. We hear the screeching of monkeys and birds. We drive a long time, climbing hills and slopes. My driver keeps reassuring me that the village is "just around the next corner". Although empty-looking, I am intrigued by the strange sight of a small hut on stilts, the highest bachelor's house in the province. A few old men, women and children move towards us, carefully and suspiciously. Everyone else has gone hunting, or is working in the fields. These people are even shyer than the tribe we visited yesterday; they run away as soon as I start to sketch. It doesn't matter; I'm fascinated by the tall hut and concentrate on my drawing. The woven plaited decoration, similar to the very sophisticated adornments of Laotian and Thai houses, is even more beautiful and intricate than that which I saw yesterday.

Return to Phnom Penh

The runway is a long stretch of ruby-red laterite and the airport is a hut with a single ticket counter. A small room is reserved for VIPs, in this case Sam Rainsy, the PSR opposition party leader, and his wife, who are taking the same plane as we are. All the other passengers are outside, standing in the heat. Our "Quiet American" is leaning against a railing, reading a book and ignoring us. My driver dropped me off at the scheduled time. I'm a bit groggy after my trip and only partially appreciate the

laughter that greets me as my three companions discover a mummified statue covered in red dust. Even after several washings my white shirt, hat and beige trousers will never quite be the same again. Apparently it's my face that's the funniest though—I'm a real red Indian.

During the flight, we spot entire sections of the forest that have been destroyed. It's a catastrophe but none of the authorities take the ecological dangers seriously. Profits are all that matter, and this deforestation is happening all over—so much so, in fact, that Cambodia is currently one of the most affected countries in Southeast Asia. The consequences are already disastrous: the land has been ruined, hundreds of species that contribute to the fragile equilibrium of the ecosystem have been destroyed, and deadly floods are becoming more and more frequent. A few Western countries are trying to alert international attention to this problem at major summits, like Kyoto. Yet Europe is one of the leading importers of wood from this region, especially the teak, which goes to make all our inexpensive living room and garden furniture.

Bang Lung airport: a wooden shed on the edge of a laterite runway.

Siem Reap

Apsara Service

We are going back to Siem Reap, by plane this time!

Sunday, 24th February

The plane for Siem Reap takes off at 7am. We leave for the airport weighed down. The three boys carry the packages, a box filled with paper towels for Benito's hotel, handmade scythes for his souvenir shop and a computer for the office. Benito carries the hard drive, Damien the screen. On arrival, we take a taxi and discover the infamous airport road lined with pompous and ugly new hotels built by Chinese or Japanese investors. They all have very similar names: Angkor this, Bayon and Apsara that, and I doubt that any tourist arriving for the first time could reach his destination if he gave the taxi driver just the hotel's name. I am moved when I recognise the Royal Pagoda, the park in front of the Grand Hotel and the roundabout where the giant portraits of King Sihanouk and Queen Monineath have temporarily disappeared. We return to our garden of Eden—Borann, l'Auberge des Temples.

Mao and Bunna greet us with big smiles. I'm happy to see them again, as well as the familiar setting: the idyllic garden, swimming pool and traditional bungalows.

"justintin" the reporter
takes the plane.

ថង់ក់អូត

ขาวนุ่ม คุ้มค่า น่าใช้
ใช้ได้ทุกโอกาส ทุกสถานที่

Song® ใหม่!พิเศษ
ใช้ครั้งเดียวทิ้ง

NEW ICE EAU DE COLOGNE TOWEL
หอมสดชื่น สะอาด ปลอดภัย

December   February
  2001   2002

There are building sites all over the
place: many investors are building
huge hotels. An extension to the airport
is under construction, as well as a
new road. the road workers are
often women. they lift baskets
full of stones that are much too
heavy for them.

147

Bunna. 21ans
យ៉ាងយន

Phalla នាង

Bunna,
the young
handicapped
receptionist
at Borann.

បុណ្ណ-ស្រីម៉ាច

Hen Sreymach

Bunna brings us a large breakfast and we chat a little. I didn't have enough time to sketch his portrait during our first trip, and I take advantage of this moment of calm. Bunna sits sideways concealing, as much as possible, his physical deformity—the misshapen humps on his back and his chest caused by bone tuberculosis he caught as a child. The illness also stunted his growth. He tells us that he fell off the roof of his house when he was one, and that the deformation dates from this accident. He didn't know his father well. He survived the Khmer Rouge epoch by hiding for several days in a ditch filled with stagnant water. His lungs suffered as a result and he became ill. He died in the 1980s. His mother is a teacher. Bunna learned English and French on his own. He looked for work in the hotel business, but no one wanted to employ a disabled person. One day he heard that Benito had just opened a hotel in Siem Reap and needed a receptionist. He took a chance and was hired immediately. Bunna has been working at Borann for over one year now. He speaks wonderfully precise, and delightfully courteous, French.

Benito has gone off to take a nap and Justin and Damien are in the pool. While I put my watercolours away, two young French women ask about our host. We introduce ourselves. Annette and Maïlys are new recruits

The multi-layer roofs at Borann, "L'Auberge des temples",

our haven of peace in the heart of Siem Reap.

148

at the Siem Reap Krousar Thmey centre. Annette arrived in early January and is here to promote the Tonle Sap exhibition and the centre's various activities. She has had brochures printed, but is facing unexpected problems with the distribution. Krousar Thmey, as a humanitarian organisation, cannot pay commissions. She is asking for free distribution but, with a few exceptions, the brochures she leaves in the hotels and guesthouses are not displayed. Another problem is that most tourists are on group tours, here for a few days and on a tight schedule. They don't have the time or inclination to discover something not included in their plans. Maïlys is a physiotherapist and works on short-term contracts. Prior to Cambodia she was in Pakistan, where she trained young, hyper-disciplined and motivated students. Here she worked hard at first but had some trouble adapting to a slower, more relaxed rhythm. The climate has something to do with this, as the heat drains all energy for several hours a day. She trains young blind people in the techniques of therapeutic massage, attempting to perfect them by adapting the skills that they already have to more specific ends.

Monday, 25th February
The Bayon. Angkor Thom

"The King suffers the pain of his subjects more than his own, which becomes an ailment of his very soul."

Jayavarman VII, who is the author of this admirable phrase and had it engraved in stone, is certainly the most fascinating and complex of all the sovereigns of Angkor. An implacable and expansionist warrior, he took revenge on the Chams for their destruction of Angkor by pursuing them into their land, the Champa. He annexed this region before moving on to conquer Annam[32], then extended his kingdom by pushing the northern and western borders even farther. He was over sixty years old when he ascended to the throne of Angkor after this victory.

On the lawns opposite the Grand Hotel.

We meet Roland Neven: a reporter and photographer who covered the war in Cambodia before being held by the Khmer rouge, with many other French nationals in the French embassy in April 1975. After a few years in the United States where he worked on the film set of Oliver Stone's "Platoon", he settled in Bangkok and opened a publishing house.

Roland Neven
2002

The Bayon,
a mountain temple
built in the heart
of the city
of Angkor Thom
by
Jayavarman VII.

A worshipper sells
incense sticks that
she plants in fragrant
bunches at the foot
of a statue of Buddha.

54 satellite towers adorned
with 216 faces of Buddha.
I linger over these enigmatic,
fleshy faces, with their almond-
shaped eyes, and well-defined,
sensual mouths, who gaze down
with compassion,
irony or
condescension?

Unified under his law, the Khmer empire then extended from Burma to the Mekong Delta and the Malaysian peninsula. He was the first king to construct so many hospitals, religious foundations and shelters for pilgrims. He also imposed Buddhism, the "wise of the wise", on his people. He identified with the Buddha so much that he had an extraordinary series of carved four-faced towers and statues created during his reign. Of limitless ambition, interested in mysticism and deeply influenced by Buddhism, he remains, to this day, a fascinating and intriguing figure—undoubtedly the most important figure in Khmer history. His people followed him in his religion and it became the common faith. Obsessed by death and immortality, Jayavarman VII built more temples than all his predecessors together. He then started the construction of his own city, Angkor Thom, built on the site of the former villa of King Udayadityavarman, near the Baphuon. He had a moat dug, 4 kilometres on each side and 100 metres wide, and a stone wall to protect the town from attack. He then built his masterpiece, the Bayon, a mountain-temple of towers sculpted with colossal faces. This was the first time that religious symbolism was accessible to the public. Previously the common man could not enter such sanctuaries, which were reserved for the king and his priests. Towards the end of his life, however, Jayavarman VII pursued his building frenzy obsessively, to the point, even, of neglecting the needs of his people. A brilliant visionary and manager, he tried to revamp the existing hydraulic system and succeeded in redesigning it to make it the most sophisticated and practical system of its kind. In addition to the Angkor Thom moat, he constructed new artificial ponds and renovated the barays[33], so that not a single drop of water would be wasted in the irrigation systems between the lakes, rivers and rice paddies. After Jayavarman's death, around 1219, Khmer art started to decline and gradually disappeared.

We had already discovered the Bayon during our first trip, when we were moved by the profound humanism of the carved faces, but this temple can be revisited endlessly, and now we are inescapably drawn back by the unique aura. It's 6:15am. The sun is slowly rising, revealing the colossal mass of the Bayon, the first rays of light sculpting the gigantic faces of Buddha. We are the first people to climb the steps and terraces leading to the towers. The discovery of a temple is a highly individual pleasure and we like to separate and lose ourselves in the labyrinth of stones, corridors and dark corners. I am fascinated by the multitude of different views offered by the omnipresent Buddhas: a change of angle or light and everything is different.

Justin found himself in a dank alcove. He had stepped over some planks blocking the entrance to the darkest galleries and sanctuaries, hidden behind collapsed stones, where he encountered only a few bats, taking flight at this intrusion. He immediately turned back, overcome by the bitter and unbearable smell of their droppings. Damien asks one of the guards, wearing a grey Mao uniform with an Apsara logo embroidered on her chest, to take a photograph of the three of us, crouching under a representation of the God-King.

Jayavarman constructed the royal terraces at the heart of Angkor Thom, just beyond the Bayon. The largest of them is the Terrace of the Elephants, some 300 metres long. It was used as a stand by the king whilst reviewing the lavish festivities held on the central square, an immense clearing. We walk along it, admiring the magnificent fresco of elephants, until we reach the central flight of steps. The handrails are supported by the trunks of three elephants crowned with lotus flowers.

The worshippers' prayers reach us from within the depths of the temples.

"And you, where do you come from?"

ទឹកបរិសុទ្ធ

Justin and Damien have wandered off on their own, enticed by Preah Palilay, a little temple whose chimney shaped forms create an almost abstract composition with the smooth, supple lines of the tree trunks.

In one of the alleys, a sign explains that cutting down a tree is like killing the spirit that inhabits it.

Ta-Nei

A very old-fashioned looking scooter parked on its own under the trees.

We notice charred holes hollowed out of several tree trunks which encourage the production of sap.

I really don't know how we've lost each other in this vast open space, but Justin and Damien have disappeared. I continue on my way along the terrace and come across a wild-looking figure, his hair tied back in a pony tail under his panama hat. Massive and determined, he walks to a certain point, holding a seemingly endless tape measure, and turns to his small, ageing Cambodian acolyte, ordering him to stretch the tape to another point. I figure out that he is an architect, only later I learn his name: Christophe Pottier, who, like Pascal Royère, supervisor of the Baphuon[34] renovations, is working on the restoration of the temples.

We leave Angkor Thom by the south gate, crossing the moat over a bridge, under the watchful eyes of fifty-four giants holding two immense Nagas. The heads and tails of the serpents stand like fans at either end. The giants are separated into two: to the left are the gods of the celestial spheres; to the right, the demons of the underworld. Symbolically linked to each other at the four gates of Angkor Thom, they represent the "Churning of the Ocean of Milk", a theme from the Indian myth of creation.

Tonight Benito has invited Kérya, the director of APSARA "Autorité pour la Protection du Site et l'Aménagement de la région d'Angkor". This state institution manages the entire Angkor site. Waiting for her to arrive, Benito shows us the photos he took from a helicopter during a trip to some temples buried deep in the forest. The aerial views are superb. Unfortunately, once they reached the sites, they were dismayed to discover that looters had recently paid the temples a visit, as there was fresh evidence of mutilation to the Devatas and doorways. Smuggling stopped during the civil war, but picked up again in 1992. Sculptures, lintels and pediments, roughly hacked off the temples, are exported via Thailand. A police unit was created in Angkor to protect this heritage, but the job is not easy, as the governments do not always help to arrest the guilty parties and middlemen. An agreement has been signed recently between Cambodia and Thailand to prevent these acts of vandalism.

CAREFULL
ELEPHANTS

We leave Angkor thom by the southern gate, and cross the walk-way over the moat, stared at by 54 giants holding two huge Nagas.

The scene symbolises the Churning of the Ocean of Milk, which gives rise to the elixir of immortality, the "Amrita".

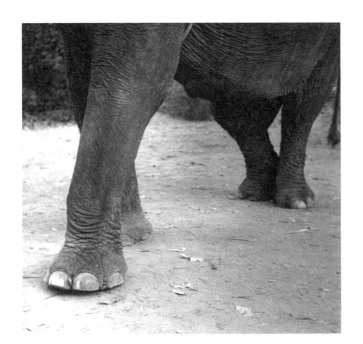

Elephants are waiting under the trees. They have been decked out with little flags, printed with the logo of a well-known American car manufacturer. Sirens soon sound and limousines arrive. A police cordon holds us back, while the MPS take their places on their new "vehicles".

The giants face each other: on the left, the "Devas", gods of the heavenly spheres, on the right the "Asuras", demons of the underworld.

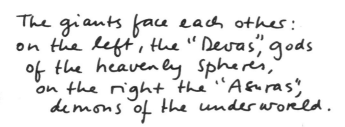

Annette, the volunteer in charge of communication, surrounded by the deaf and blind children from the Krousar Thmey center in Siem Reap.

Lina, the blind children's attractive, but melancholic, teacher.

LYNA-KNANI ້ง่·ฉ่จ่ง
teacher of the blind children
KROUSAR THMEY IN SIEMREAP
CAMBODIA

The Krousar Thmey centre in Siem Reap is in a good location, opposite the Jayavarman VII children's hospital and on the road to the temples. Devoted to deaf and blind children, this centre is one of largest and most beautiful. We had already accompanied the school pick-up run at dawn in Battambang and now we wanted to take the youngsters home after school. I sit in the front with the driver and one of the teachers; Damien and Justin follow on a motorbike. The truck raises clouds of red dust, forcing the boys to remain at a respectful distance. Justin gets in the back of the truck at the first stop; the children are delighted. Comfortably enclosed in the front cabin with the air conditioning on full blast, I chat with the teacher, squeezed beside me. She is slender and pretty but has a sad expression, and a kind of weariness occasionally crosses her face. Thirty years old, she was one of the first Krousar Thmey teachers for blind children. She had been working as a professor in a public school and then followed a specific training eight years ago to teach Braille. The first time she met her class she was so shocked by their miserable condition that she cried for two days. In Cambodia, where one in four children dies before the age of five, and where people struggle hard to survive, a disabled child is considered a dead weight for a family, being just another mouth to feed. Plonked in a corner of the house, such a child is left to grow like a weed, isolated from the family and with no chance of attending school. Alone and inactive, they often retreat into silence, developing the pathology of autism. Krousar Thmey first had to, literally, tame these children, treat their trauma and gently re-educate them. Lina tells me that she is not married but that she is financially independent. Her family comes from Kompong Cham and Phnom Penh. Her father is a farmer and her mother a teacher. We drop off the last child, a deaf

" School's out! "

eight-year-old boy. His mother is waiting for him on her bicycle and Lina is always moved to see her collecting her son every day, while all the other children walk home.

Talking to Benito, back at Borann, I learn more about the melancholic Lina. She is actually divorced, after a forced marriage to a man she didn't love. This has changed her status within her family and society at large. It will be hard for her to remarry.

It's late afternoon, the city is unusually noisy with the monotonous sound of prayers booming from loud-speakers. Over the last two days, a rumour has been going around town that a "venerable" monk is to be cremated tonight, under the full moon, at Wat Enkosar. On the way, we stop at the École Française d'Extrême-Orient, home to the architects working on the temple restorations. Benito wants us to meet Pascal Royère, the chief architect for the last seven years on the Baphuon site. He studied in Syria before being sent to Cambodia. His wife, Andrée, is a botanist and is drawing up an inventory of all the trees and plants she finds. She flips through the pages of her large notebooks, showing me her collection. She tries to find the former use and the symbolism for each species. She travels to distant villages, where people still use herbal remedies and can recall the beliefs associated with certain plants. While I talk with her, Pascal looks over our sketchbooks. It seems as if he'll let us visit the Baphuon building site. Tomorrow is impossible though, because it's pay day. The 150 workers receive their wages in cash. It's a ritual that takes several hours. A pick-up truck, protected by guards with Kalachnikovs, brings in wads of banknotes. There's also a certain amount of tension on these days, as robberies are still common throughout this country, which has a long tradition of banditry. Jacques Théron had told us about two thieves who locked three of his workers in a hut. To make sure they didn't escape the bandits simply nailed their hands and feet to the floor. The author Jean Delvert discusses a scene he witnessed in 1950 when a village of more than 200 people was terrorised by two barely armed bandits. He explains this phenomenon by "the absence of any real village structure, by apathy and fear. But also it's an outlet for Khmer violence, which is masked and contained by Buddhism".

Cremation of a monk

A dense crowd prevents us from getting any closer to the pagoda. The holy site, which is so calm and reverent during the day, has been transformed into a gigantic carnival. In the middle, behind the rows of cheap music stands, our gaze is drawn towards the terrace, where a canopy blazing with thousands of fairy lights covers the coffin. A firecracker hidden inside a dragon's head suspended from a rack above will trigger the fire, beginning the cremation. Seated on the ground behind a rope, the devoted, dressed all in white, bow and pray. A group of monks of all ages, their robes forming a block of brilliant orange, stands on the other side of the brightly illuminated pagoda. Everyone is looking towards the three venerable monks sitting, in order of importance, in armchairs on the terrace. The crowd presses in from all sides. Damien tries to take a photograph by holding his camera above his head, but Benito stops him immediately. It's considered a sacrilege and he has already heard a few insults and hostile remarks directed our way. In fact, we are practically the only barangs[35] present. We don't feel like waiting for another two hours in this suffocating crowd. We return to our motorcycles and Benito takes us to his favourite restaurant, the Soup Dragon.

THE SOUP DRAGON

Christophe left London and the financial world for two years off travelling the real world. He met Benito and settled in Siem Reap, where he set up a centre for street children.

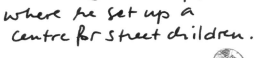

When they got married, the Vietnamese owner and her English husband asked their guests for donations to Krousar Thmey rather than wedding presents. Christophe joins us. He met Benito a year ago, during his sabbatical year. Aware of the growing problem of homeless children, he proposed the creation of a project in Siem Reap. Happy and excited, he announces that he has just found a place to house the children and a living space for himself on the first floor of a lovely traditional house, just behind Borann. A group of boys walk by, all in a terrible state. Benito asks the owner to serve them something to eat. The Soup Dragon is one of the few restaurants that will serve the street children. All the others chase them away. He demands that they eat while he watches: often those who carry their food off just toss it away up the street because the glue they've sniffed ruins their appetite. In less than six months, they lose their minds, wasting away and roaming the pavements in agony. It's a recent phenomenon reaching Cambodia from Thailand, along with Ecstasy and other illegal substances. The NGOs are already overwhelmed and are somewhat powerless to do anything about it.

We notice a band of stars in the sky. These are not celestial bodies, but lighted helium balloons connected together by string. Each contains a prayer and a wish, sent heavenwards so that they may come true.

Wednesday, 27th February
A colonial dinner

Nathalie Ridel and Jean-Pierre Martials' house is also situated close to the pagoda where the monk was cremated, but the usual evening calm has returned. The strident loudspeakers are quiet and the hot, heavy night only hums with the buzz of insects and the sound of rustling leaves. Bathed in a subtle golden light, the house reveals the pure lines and discreet opulence of true Cambodian style. The immense wooden floor has been

One of the sculpture workshops of the "Chantiers Écoles d'Angkor," run by Jean-Pierre Martial and Nathalie Ridel. Their ambition is to revive traditional arts and crafts among the younger generations.

Nat. SAVON

polished to a shiny lustre, the mahogany gleams warmly. A young Cambodian approaches with tiny steps, restricted by the straight cut of her impeccably folded sarong; the woven silk has a bee pattern that shimmers with reddish-brown reflections. She stands behind two young children, a boy and girl who have come to say goodnight before going to bed. Nathalie asks us to sit down. Her pretty face, framed with brown wavy locks, evokes a 1920s beauty, an image described with subtle sensuality by George Groslier in his melancholic descriptions of colonial Cambodia. The table is set on the terrace and glitters with scented candles, whose flames are reflected as tiny sparkles on the plates and glasses.

Jean-Pierre moved to Cambodia about ten years ago. He created, and has developed, the "Chantiers-Écoles d'Angkor", a French-sponsored project that has gradually become his own private company. These workshops train adolescents in traditional Khmer arts and crafts, including wood and stone sculpture, painting and silk weaving. The students are all teenagers from poor families, some are even homeless, and the goal of the workshops is not only an attempt at social rehabilitation for these children, but also to train them in a noble and lucrative trade. The pre-selection is rigorous, however, as the high reputation of the objects created in the workshops demands disciplined, and extremely motivated, students. Jean-Pierre met Nathalie when she was sent by the Cambodian Culture Ministry to draw up an inventory of traditional techniques that were still practised in post-war Cambodia. They worked together to promote the workshop schools, motivated by a shared passion for Khmer culture and convinced that their project would be a humanitarian necessity. Today, they are famous throughout the world and orders flow in for

On the ground, one of the apprentices sands down a head of Jayavarman VII.

monumental sculptures and decorative projects. In fact, they have just completed work on the newest luxury hotel in Siem Reap, the Pansea, decorated entirely by their craftsmen in a traditional style, using Cambodia's most beautiful materials. An inaugural ceremony was held this morning, attended by Prime Minister Hun Sen, who was accompanied by a few ministers and an official delegation. Jean-Pierre admits that he is exasperated with these celebrations at which certain high-level civil servants take all the credit for other people's work, having stuck a spanner in along the way.

Nathalie, at the other end of the table, recalls a few childhood memories. Her Cambodian father ran the Pasteur Institute in Phnom Penh. Her French mother was a teacher. Nathalie remembers clearly the sound of sirens and bombings. Their teachers would order them to get under their desks or send them home at the double. They were finally repatriated in 1974, just before the Khmer Rouge captured Phnom Penh. Only a small number of her father's family was able to leave the country. All the others were flung into the turmoil. Descendants of wealthy, intellectual families and holding important jobs, they were the first targets of the Khmer Rouge, who decided to rid the nation of the entire

The classrooms of the "Chantiers Écoles" are formed around a vast courtyard.

educated urban class, accused of belonging to a capitalist bourgeoisie. Her uncle, a pilot and flight-captain, managed to conceal his identity in the camps, passing as a simple peasant. He was almost discovered in 1977, some three years after having been forced out of Phnom Penh. The man working alongside him in the rice paddies looked up, following the path of an aeroplane. He simply asked, "I wonder what it feels like to be up there?" Nathalie's uncle was about to reply, "I know, I was a pilot," when he stopped himself in time. It was just as well, as it turned out that his colleague was an informer and had denounced several of his comrades. This was an atrocious period. Everyone mistrusted everybody else, even the children were indoctrinated by the Khmer Rouge to denounce their parents. Any sign of kindness was considered suspicious.

Friday, 1st March
Work on the Baphuon site

Pascal Royère told us to meet him at 7am, when the workers start their day on the site. An EFEO panel marks the entrance. A shed stores the tractors and other machine tools. Numbered stones are scattered on the ground all around us and under the trees. There are more than 300,000 of them, all carved by the builders of King Udayarman, who decided in the eleventh century to construct this colossal work. The Khmer empire was at the peak of its power at that time.

We climb to the top of a slope that takes us to the first level of the mountain-temple, where we find the hut housing the architects' offices. A man from Brittany greets us; he is the site foreman and one of Pascal Royère's colleagues. Before explaining the ongoing work to us, he suggests we tour the site to get a feel for it. He hands us over to one of his workers, who guides us on a reconnaissance tour. Approximately 150 workers have been employed full-time for seven years. They include

164

A stone cutter reconstitutes the missing pieces of a frieze, millimetre by millimetre.

Jean-Claude Prigent,
a Breton of Irish stock
and Pascal Royère's
foreman.

When it's time for a break, the workers
sit on the white hot steps where
the temperature's nearly 40 degrees,
sheltering under sloping panels that
they've made of woven palms, propped up
by bamboo stems.

ÉCOLE FRANÇAISE
D'EXTRÊME-ORIENT

Each of the thousands of stones that make up the Baphuon has been identified and numbered on charts, displayed in the architects' hut.

166

stonecutters, masons, crane operators and drivers for the various vehicles: tractors, bulldozers and strange carts used to transport the stones concealed in the undergrowth. I sit down on a ledge over the entrance, above the bridge that once led to the eastern facade of the temple. Five workers are standing around a solid piece of sandstone, while another one measures it. With their red and yellow construction helmets, they look like Playmobil figures. A stonecutter on scaffolding is re-creating the missing piece of a frieze. Working with a hammer and chisel, he sculpts the new piece of sandstone set into a slot in the old, continuing his precise work milimetre by milimetre. He comes from the "Chantiers Ecoles d'Angkor", which provides the EFEO with the best stonecutters of the younger generation. The air rings with the clinking sounds we heard as we approached the Baphuon, as if a flock of woodpeckers had replaced the cicadas. There is a striking contrast between the meticulous work of these carvers and the workers who handle the enormous blocks of stone.

The heat has risen quickly and, by 10am, time for the morning break, it's almost 40 degrees centigrade on the white-hot steps of the Baphuon. Pascal Royère invites us into his office for a drink to help us re-hydrate. On the wall, next to the coat-rack hung with an array of helmets, caps and bob hats, he deciphers the various plans and drawings of the Baphuon, illustrating the successive phases of restoration. One of the drawings is particularly fascinating: each stone of the immense mountain-temple is drawn and numbered. As the temple is reconstructed, the foremen go out to the stone cemetery and pick out the one that corresponds to the stone on the drawing. The new Baphuon building site was inaugurated in 1995, after a twenty-five-year break. All the drawings made by the illustrious predecessors of the EFEO had disappeared under the Khmer Rouge. Patrick Cerales, a computer graphics specialist, managed to identify eight hundred different shapes of stone.

Pascal Royère, who gained precious experience in Syria, is in charge of the Baphuon site. Seven years of titanic work.

The workers' cloakroom

At Preah Kahn, one of the most imposing and beautiful of Angkor's temples. We're alone, apart from two guards who are sweeping up dead leaves.
Justin nicknames them "Black & White"!

He created a three-dimensional reconstruction of the original temple's architecture on-screen. The work is scheduled to finish by 2003, but Pascal doesn't think they will meet this deadline and hopes to obtain an extension until 2005, along with the necessary funding, of course. Surrounded by young Khmer architects, he is now taking on the major project, an immense Buddha, 60 metres long, reclining on its side and taking up the temple's entire western facade to a depth of five metres. He had to dismantle it completely to reinforce it with a concrete shell that acts as a framework under its "skin" of stones. For the time being, only the head and part of the bust have been re-constructed.

Saturday, 2ⁿᵈ March
The silk village

Pheanuroth is a prince of the Sisowath lineage that ruled until the death of King Monivong in 1941. The French governor of Indochina then placed the young Norodom Sihanouk on the throne; he was just nineteen years old and a successor from a related branch of the family. France took this decision thinking it could more easily manipulate the young king. This turned out to be a major error of judgement, for which they would pay heavily.

Taking refuge in France, Pheanuroth pursued his studies and married a French woman. He continued working there until the Paris peace agreements were signed in 1991, when he decided, as did many exiled Cambodians, to return to his country and help with its reconstruction. For several years he's worked on an ambitious government project, encouraging and promoting traditional arts and crafts through training programmes and a regional relocation of each activity. He took charge of the silk trade, managing and overseeing each step from the planting of mulberry bushes to the final woven fabric. The initial investments were extremely large. Villagers, particularly women, had to be

170

Pheanuroth, a prince of the Sisowath lineage, heads a vast government project to restore local crafts.

Unwinding silk cocoons.

After gorging themselves on mulberry leaves, the silk worms are placed in twigs where they start spinning their cocoons.

The spinners use bicycle wheels to wind the thread round the spool.

trained, but he also had to provide the raw materials, the plants, the worms and the spinning and weaving equipment. The supporting set-up programme is scheduled to last two years. The village must then be able to take over the activity, becoming self-sufficient and, hopefully, making a profit. Another of his underlying aims is to put a stop to the exodus of young people towards the cities, where they often end up in miserable and overcrowded conditions in slum neighbourhoods.

We were able to contact Pheanuroth thanks to one of Justin's connections in France. After a first meeting, he offered to show us a silk village, located about 70 kilometres from Siem Reap. The rendez-vous is set for 7am Saturday morning at Borann, where he'll come to get us in a 4 x 4 with his driver. Our time is very limited now, as we are soon returning to France. Damien opts to stay in Siem Reap with Christophe, following the homeless children project. Benito and the lovely Maïlys, however, come along with us. Since the start of the trip I've been accompanied by my three male companions, with their own particular sense of humour, so I appreciate the presence of Maïlys. The trip seems short and pleasant, although we've been driving for two hours on a terrible road. We leave the main road and, after a few kilometres, reach the village. The houses are crowded around a main street, which is just a sandy track in the forest. Everything is calm and peaceful. The traditional houses, with airy verandas, are surrounded by small gardens and the only things out of place are the discarded plastic bags. A woman and a group of children accompany us to a meadow, where the young mulberry bushes have just been planted. Nearby oblong wooden huts, with grating on the doors and windows, contain the precious silkworms. They come from Cambodia or Thailand. The latter produces a more regular, and more importantly a larger quantity of, silk. The worms are placed on screens lined with mulberry leaves. They devour the leaves for several days until they are ready to

The spinners' and weavers' workshops are set up under the houses away from the heat.

MASSAGE

Maïlys, a physiotherapist who recently arrived to train blind youngsters in therapeutic massage, discovers the peaceful, yet industrious, life of a remote village at the same time as we do.

weave their cocoons. They are then placed in boxes divided into sections or, more traditionally, placed in a knotted sheaf of suspended twigs. After a week, the yellowish ivory-coloured cocoons are gathered just before the chrysalis metamorphoses into a butterfly and dropped in a pot of boiling water. At this point, a spinner, equipped with a strainer and a pair of tweezers, picks up the threads of several cocoons and gathers them together using a winding machine mounted on a wooden frame. The thread is so fine that several are twined together to form a sufficiently strong and regular thread. This is then formed into skeins, or rolled onto large spools for weaving. Warping frames, although used by everyone, are very expensive for a village. The organisation provides one per community and appoints a village elder to be responsible for its maintenance. This person also oversees the entire silk-making process. The spinners work on elevated plat-forms under the houses. With their babies nearby, and a pile of soft pale gold yarn at hand, the natural colour of silk, the young women spin, using a bobbin, each move-ment of their arms twirling the wheel encircled with a loop of shiny thread. A few metres away, in front of another house, the skeins are dipped in buckets filled with dyes. As we pursue our exploration, we discover all the women working together around magnificent traditional looms. Grandmothers, mothers and young girls all participate and play a specific role in the process. Silk production has

I'm fascinated not so much by the finger movements as by the toes, like tiny puppets that activate the pedals at top speed.

Beat Richner, a swiss paediatrician runs three hospitals that take children in, giving them fee treatment. He's also an amateur cellist, who calls himself "Beatocello" and gives a twice-weekly concert.

One of the many mothers waiting her turn at the entrance to the hospital.

become the second source of revenue after rice growing, and keeps the women busy all year, except when the rice has to be planted and harvested, and every villager, regardless of their age or social standing, works day and night in the paddies.

Beatocello

Every time we drive to the temples we go past a large building with pink plaster walls. We noticed it right away because of the immense head of Jayavarman VII that stands on the roof, protected by a small wooden shelter. It is, surprisingly, not a hotel but an ultra-modern hospital, created by a Swiss paediatrician, Beat Richner. This doctor first discovered Cambodia when he worked in the country between 1974-75 as an assistant at the Kantha Bopha children's hospital, constructed by King Sihanouk. He had to leave the country when the Khmer Rouge took over and could only return in 1991 as a visitor. One year later, he re-opened the former hospital, followed by the Kantha Bopha II in 1996. The Siem Reap hospital was then constructed in 1999, and named after Jayavarman VII. Beat Richner is one of Cambodia's most charismatic figures: every year his hospital treats, free of charge, over 50,000 children under the age of fourteen. This age limit had to be set so that the establishments could be properly administered. They posess all the latest medical technology and equipment. He answers his detractors, who criticise his practice as overly expensive "luxury doctoring", by saying that it's not possible to heal people with cheap medicines. He rejects the idea that third-world children shouldn't have access to the same treatment as Westerners. Driven by an iron will and an extraordinary energy, Beat Richner even performs on stage in support of his beliefs. An amateur cellist and composer, he plays for tourists on Wednesday and Saturday nights in the conference rooms of the Siem Reap hospital, transforming himself into "Beatocello".

Kronsar thmey also teaches
the children the art of
shadow theatre, from making
the puppets to manipulating
them. The day before we leave
we watch a wonderful show,
improvised by our young hosts.

The concert starts at 7:15pm, and Justin and I have decided to attend. Tonight, the entrance is clear of the usual line of families, sitting on the pavement waiting for news of their sick children. Only mothers are allowed inside, where they can stay day and night by their child's bedside. We walk down a white corridor decorated with black-and-white photographs, poignant portraits of the sick children posing alongside Beat Richner and the hospital staff. We take our places as Beatocello rushes onto the stage, head bowed, removes his cello from the case, sits and finally looks at the audience. A stubborn and energetic figure, he introduces himself briefly and immediately starts to play, beginning with classical pieces. Once the audience is caught up in the atmosphere, he attacks the core of his performance, radical protest songs, that explain his convictions and sweep away all preconceived ideas about medical programmes in the third world. He vents his anger: for him, the primary health problem in Cambodia is not famine or mines, as most tourists think, but tuberculosis. The authorities and the NGOs play down the problem because the treatment, and necessary structures, is far too expensive. They tell him that children should wash their hands and learn to eat correctly! "It's absurd! You can wash your hands for hours, but it's not going to solve the problem. Everyone has spent far too long ignoring the menace of tuberculosis in this country. Each year we detect 10,000 new cases!" He is flamboyant and authoritative, but also, his detractors would add, intolerant and a megalomaniac. It doesn't matter. This man, who is totally devoted to his cause, radiates so much energy, and such heartfelt sincerity, that we are impressed and deeply moved.

From the edge
of one of the
towers of
Angkor Wat,
I admire the beautiful
sandstone Deratas, alchemized
an orangey-gold by a ray of sunshine.

Over 2000 Apsaras
and Deratas adorn the
walls of Angkor Wat.

zen
Go'5u

Sunset over Angkor Wat is a
tourist cliché that we've
tried to avoid until now.
But we can't go back to France
without saying goodbye to
the temples. The walk way
is obstructed by a motley crew
of tourists of all nationalities,
but the lawns are deserted,
except for a herd of cows
that wander nonchalantly
around.

A novice monk
on a pilgrimage.

Angkor Wat
is still a
place of worship.

and of pilgrimage
for Cambodians,
be they lay people,
worshippers or monks.

A joyful band of novice monks hangs
on to the only ramp that facilitates
the climb to the central towers.

Vertigo sufferers beware!

A Visit To The Queen

Dressed to the nines, Justin poses with his patriotic scarf!

A visit to the queen at the Royal Palace

A surprise awaits us on our return to Phnom Penh. The director of protocol has just called Benito to tell him that the king cannot meet with us, but that Queen Monineath will honour us with an audience tomorrow, at IIam on the dot.

Benito rummages through his library and returns with a pile of books to refresh our memories about the king's reign and his most glorious period from 1955 to 1969, the Sangkum Reastr Niyum. The destiny of King Sihanouk, violently criticised by some, praised by others, still intrigues and fascinates biographers and observers. After embodying all the contradictions and excesses of his country, he managed to survive the turmoil, unscathed, and reclaim the throne, to the acclaim of his people. Although his power is now only symbolic, he continues to represent the legitimacy of Cambodian royalty and is, without any doubt, an important factor of unity and stability in Cambodia today, acting as a buffer between the fratricidal rivalries of the political parties.

He is a multifaceted, ambitious, eclectic and brilliant figure: he is the monarch that proclaimed independence and threw out the French, then abdicated to govern as head of his political party, and he is a reformer and visionary who wished to modernise his country to rival Western nations. A man of power, he is also a man of seduction, with many conquests to his name; he's an avid fan of cinema—so much so, in fact, that he left the throne for a time to become a director and produced several films as well. Yet history caught up with him, and he was forced into exile in Beijing, where he chose the anti-American camp. Ironically, after supporting the Khmer Rouge, he was called back to Phnom Penh and kept under house arrest for five years, while the Angkar soldiers assassinated both his family and his people. Seeking refuge once again in China, prior to the Vietnamese invasion, he never gave up and continued to operate clandestinely in his country's politics, patiently waiting his turn. After the Paris agreements in 1991, he finally returned to Cambodia and claimed his role as king.

Benito wakes us up early. He wants us to have plenty of time to get ready. He checks our clothes: my dress and the suits, ties and freshly polished shoes of the boys. He also gives us a few additional tips concerning palace etiquette: address the queen as "Your Majesty", not "Your Highness", which is a lesser title; never speak before she does and never interrupt; don't make any sudden movements, or one of her infamous Korean bodyguards will pounce without warning. We try to take all these details on board as our stage fright mounts.

We present ourselves at the "Gate of Victory" at 10:50am. We see the escort motorcycle waiting for us just beyond the entrance. A guard comes out to check our papers before opening the gate. We pass through and wait a few more minutes for the motorcyclist to receive an order, via walkie-talkie, to start up. We then cross the

We arrive early and wait
in the cool of the car, watching
the comings and goings
of the "cyclo-pousse".

gardens, around various pavilions and pagodas, as far as the entrance to the Preah[36] Tineang Tevea Vinicchay, which houses the palace reception rooms. A squadron of major-domos and bodyguards awaits us at the base of a large staircase. The director of protocol, Madame Khek Sysoda, takes us into an antechamber where the queen, standing, is waiting for us with a smile.

Benito greets her first, bowing deeply with his hands joined as if in prayer. I perform the same reverence. A photographer captures these moments. We follow her into a large white and gilded reception room. I'm a little disappointed to see that it's decorated in Western style. I am placed, with Benito, to the queen's right. Justin and Damien sit to her left, with the director of protocol. The bodyguards have disappeared behind some columns. Her Majesty the Queen is the king's sixth wife and the only one who holds the title. Daughter of a Franco-Italian father and a Cambodian mother, she has given him two children, Prince Sihamoni and Prince Narindrapong. She speaks a faultless French, expressing with regret that her husband cannot receive us personally. She gives his age as the reason: he has just turned eighty, is in frail health and only goes out for major events. She also alluded briefly to his suspicion of Western journalists. Despite his professed respect and his fondness for France, where all his children were educated, he has been especially hurt on several occasions, by virulent, and he believes unfair, criticism made by French intellectuals, who ignore all the social and economic improvements he's made for his country.

They both appreciated our gift, a copy of the book *Zanzibar*, an island they visited in the 1970s, invited by the Tanzanian president, Julius Nyerere. Queen Monineath gives us a gift from the king, a book about the Royal Palace, and another about the Sangkum Reastr Niyum. Then she suddenly relaxes and asks us questions about our stay in Cambodia. We tell her about our trip to Kratie and Ratanakiri, while I turn the pages of my sketchbook.

181

She laughs at the stories of our adventures, lamenting the road conditions and also the deforestation. She also regrets that so few Cambodian women use contraceptives. Too many children are born, condemned to live in misery. She admits that she and her husband are extremely isolated and cannot do much for their country. "The king suffers from this, as he is above all 'the Father King', father of his people, and he worries now, at the end of his life, about the future of his children". To our surprise, as Benito advised us not to mention the taboo subject of the Khmer Rouge period, she brings it up herself, calling it "the black era". She and her husband were kept as desperate and powerless prisoners inside the walls of the palace for five years, until 1979, when they learned that the Vietnamese would reach the city the following day. They expected to die, but at the last minute some men came to get them and put them on a plane sent by China. She stressed the fact that despite their forced exile, the king always retained a contact with his country and, especially, his people. They frequently travelled to the refugee camps on the Thai border, where they met Benito. Ever since, they have followed his work and supported his projects, aware of the difficulties he has faced and overcome, particularly during the early years.

The queen stands up and officially gives Benito an envelope containing 2,000 dollars for Krousar Thmey, while a cameraman films the scene. Returning to the subject of our book, she expresses her delight that we did not limit our trip to a visit of the monuments, but also showed interest in rural Cambodia, and the daily lives of the population. She almost seems to envy us, as we continue to tell her about our travels, that we have been able to see and do so much in such a short period of time. She only leaves the palace for official occasions, such as inaugurations and commemorations. All these activities are scheduled long in advance and are subjected to the approval of the protocol office. The "unexpected" is a notion that disappeared from her life long ago. She looks back with nostalgia on a boat trip upon Lake Tonle Sap. And she still laughs at the memory of a visit by Princess Margaret and her husband, the photographer Anthony Armstrong Jones. The entire staff was in a tizzy when the latter suddenly disappeared from the palace. He had only wanted to go for a walk and returned two hours later carrying a hammock he'd purchased in a nearby street. How well she understood him!

We have been talking for almost an hour with the queen. The director of protocol makes a discreet sign, which Her Majesty notices. She stands up gracefully, thanking us for our visit that allowed her to travel beyond the walls of her palace. Vivacious and friendly, she accompanies us to the entrance and gently pushes aside my out-stretched hand to kiss me on both cheeks. We take our leave, totally under the spell of her charm, simplicity and kindness.

The "Portal of Victory", the Royal Palace

ROYAUME DU CAMBODGE

ព្រះរាជាណាចក្រកម្ពុជា

Two stamps issued for King Sihanouk's eightieth birthday, celebrating the glories of his youth.

a somptuous pagoda leading to and the gardens.

The farewell meal

For our final lunch at "La Casa", Benito orders a feast from the cook, Ya. We watch her come and go as she unloads her baskets full of glistening fish, vegetables and other ingredients she bought at the market. Squatting on the ground, with several bowls in front of her, she grinds all sorts of coloured spices. She removes the scales and cuts the fish at the last moment, then places the pieces in wide and shiny banana leaves. I regret I don't follow the complex preparations for our surprise meal more carefully. We have to pack our bags and wrap up all the precious gifts we bargained for at the Russian market: silks and kramas, statues and other small objects, cards, old stamps, jewels and trinkets, which we'll distribute among our friends at home, offering a glimpse of Cambodia.

The meal is ready. The small, joyful community of "La Casa" is waiting for us. Especially Thary, who's holding a videocassette. He tells us that he saw us on the television news last night, when they broadcast our visit to the queen for over five minutes! He recorded the programme and has already sent someone to make three copies. Ya carefully places green packages, folded and tied, on our plates: this is her surprise for us. Amok is ground fish mixed with a pot-pourri of spices and cooked in coconut milk, braised and served in a banana leaf, a feast for all the senses. For dessert she has prepared another favourite dish, smaller banana leaf packages, containing a translucent paste stuffed with coconut and large pink sweet beans. Served with black coffee, they melt in our mouths with a subtle sweet and sour sensation.

I listen to Benito and Thary; they are discussing their plans for the forthcoming days and weeks. I feel sad, because by this time tomorrow we'll be very far from Cambodia. I don't like being apart from what I've devoted my heart and soul to during our two trips here. However, there's the book to think about, and the happy prospect of spending at least one or two years in a "time bubble", transforming our memories into the story of a voyage and a passion.

In one month's time, for the Khmer New Year, the 1,500 children, and their 190 teachers, will come together from all the Krousar Thmey centres to celebrate the anniversary of the "new Cambodian family". This is a truly prodigious generation of children, their faces lit up with vitality and innocence. The future of their country is in their hands and, hopefully, they will be able to transcend their tragic heritage. Gods and monsters stand side by side on the steps of Angkor in an eternal battle between heaven and hell, good and evil. As the heirs to the God-Kings, it is now the children's turn to stand guard over this fragile balance.

For the Khmer new year, Krousar Thmey
celebrated its anniversary by bringing
the 1500 children, and their 190 teachers,
together in front of Angkor Wat.

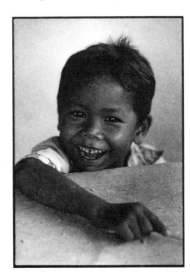

The history of Cambodia starts with the creation of Fou Nan, a rich and powerful state located in the Mekong Delta. It was influenced by Indian civilisation and extended its domination until the sixth century.

Fou Nan was overthrown by a vassal state, the Tchen-La, a name used by the Chinese to designate Cambodia until the thirteenth century.

The so-called Angkor period extended from the seventh to the thirteenth century and included an extraordinary dynasty of Khmer sovereigns, who built countless temples and cities.

The early fourteenth century saw the decline of the Khmer empire. Annam and then Siam ruled over the Khmers until the nineteenth century.

1860: The naturalist Henri Mouhot discovers the ruins of Angkor.

1863: King Norodom I signs a treaty making Cambodia a French protectorate.

1887: Creation of the Indochinese Union, setting up a direct French administration controlling the protectorate.

1907: Franco-Siamese treaty returning the provinces of Battambang, Sisophon and Siem Reap to Cambodia.

1941: Representatives of the Vichy regime place the 19-year-old Prince Norodom Sihanouk on the throne.

1953: Independence of Cambodia. King Norodom Sihanouk becomes head of state. The French are defeated at Dien Bien Phu, and Vietnam is divided in two, according to the terms of the Geneva agreement. This is the end of French Indochina.

1960: Sihanouk proclaims Cambodian neutrality, but, remaining suspicious of the Thais and South Vietnamese, he looks for support from China and North Vietnam.

1965: The United States sends ground troops in to protect South Vietnam from the communist invasion. Formation of the Khmer communist movement, supported by Beijing, taking the name Khmer Communist Party (KCP).

1966: The right wing wins the legislative elections and forms a government under Lon Nol, who is hostile to Sihanouk.

1969–73: America bombs eastern Cambodia with B52s, using defoliants, destroying villages and killing many civilians.

1970: A coup d'état in Phnom Penh, while Sihanouk is travelling in France. General Lon Nol proclaims the Khmer Republic and calls on the United States for support. The King takes refuge in Beijing. American and South Vietnamese troups invade Cambodia, while the Khmer Rouge becomes a major fighting force in the countryside.

1973: The Paris Peace Agreements are signed and American soldiers withdraw from Vietnam. The KCP forcibly enlists young Cambodian peasants in the Revolutionary Army of Liberation.

1975: The Khmer Rouge enter Phnom Penh on April 17th. In 48 hours, they empty the capital of all its residents, forcing them to work in the rice paddies. This is the start of an ethnic cleansing campaign, "the killing fields", that affects every level of the population and lasts for four years. The torture centre, Tuol Sleng, opens in Phnom Penh.

1975–79: Pol Pot's regime transforms the country, which is renamed Democratic Kampuchea, into a gigantic concentration camp. Nearly two million Cambodians (one in four) die violently from illness or malnutrition. China provides the totality of financial support for the state of Kampuchea.

1979: Major Vietnamese offensive and capture of Phnom Penh on January 7th.

1979: Cambodia's hereditary enemies "liberate" the country and form a government, the "People's Republic of Kampuchea". Khmer forces fall apart due to famine, and their leaders retreat to Thailand. The military forces form guerrilla units in the forest along the Thai border. Boycotted by the international community, Cambodia is cut off from the rest of the world until 1989.

1982: Sihanouk heads an opposition coalition that includes the Khmer Rouge.

1991: International peace agreement signed in Paris. In principle it ends the civil war. Many Khmer Rouge defect after the United Nations–led elections. Several months later Khmer Rouge forces return to guerrilla warfare.

1992: Nearly 400,000 refugees living in camps on the Thai border return to the country.

1993: First free elections. Former enemies Ranariddh, King Sihanouk's son, and Hun Sen, a former Vietnamese ally, share power. Both are named prime minister, with two ministers for each position, representing the two movements: Ranariddh's Funcinpec and Hun Sen's PPC. Sihanouk is named Cambodia's constitutional sovereign.

1996: Massive desertions from the Khmer Rouge, led by Ieng Sary. Pol Pot's former associate, isolated in the Pailin region, finally adheres to the peace movement and signs an agreement with Hun Sen.

1997: Hun Sen overthrows Ranariddh, ending the fragile ruling coalition. Manoeuvring to divide and eliminate his political adversaries, Hun Sen manages to legitimise his coup d'état and impose himself as head of Cambodia and his ruling party, the PPC.

1998: Death of Pol Pot and collapse of the Khmer Rouge movement.

Until today, and despite international pressure, no tribunal has yet been created to judge the war crimes of the Khmer Rouge leaders.

Sisamouth Sim, singing legend who died at Thol Sleng.

Glossary

1. krama: traditional cotton print cloth worn in a number of ways (scarf, loincloth and turban) by all Cambodians.

2. Phnom Penh: phnom means mountain or hill in Khmer. Phnom Penh means the hill of Penh. According to legend, an old woman named Penh discovered four images of Buddha on the banks of the Mekong; she then placed them on a nearby hill and the city grew up around them.

3. Psar Thmei: psar means market in Khmer. In this case, it refers to the New Market, also known as the Central Market.

4. Wat Lang Ka: wat means the grounds and buildings of a pagoda. This temple, located near the Independence Monument, was the second wat to be restored after 1979.

5. George Groslier (1887-1945) created the National Museum of Cambodia and was its first curator. A scientist, ethnologist, illustrator and author, he dedicated his entire life to Cambodia, which he loved with a passion, and was devoted to its art, history and archaeology, as well as to the people and the country's traditions and culture.

6. Russian market: so named as the Russians, who were in Cambodia supporting the Vietnamese from 1979 to 1989, could find products from their country here. Since, it has become popular with foreigners, expatriates, NGOs and tourists.

7. Sambor Prei Kuk: capital of the Chenla kingdom in the early seventh century.

8. Kompong Kdei bridge: kompong means riverbank-village in Khmer.

9. Laterite: coarse-grained, red, iron-bearing stone, widely used in the construction of temples, being local and easy to work.

10. Nagas: snakes associated with mythical divinities. They are represented as cobras with multiple heads. They are the masters of water and the earth, the guardians of wealth.

11. Brahma: the creative deity in Hinduism. He is represented with four faces and is generally holding a rosary, an ewer, or sometimes a spectrum and a bow.

12. Shiva: a supreme deity in Hinduism widely worshipped in Cambodia. In the Hindu trinity, Shiva is the "destructive" God that controls life and death.

13. Vishnu: a supreme deity in Hinduism. In the trinity, he is the protector who battles to save the universal order.

14. Ramayana: name of one of the versions of a major Indian and Southeast Asian epic poem. It tells of the earthly adventures of Rama, an incarnation of Vishnu. Rapa, the incarnation of evil, has stolen Rama's wife. He then forms an army of monkeys to free his wife. The Khmer version is the Rama-kirti, "the glory of Rama".

15. Chams: members of an Indonesian-speaking ethnic tribe that lived on the coast of central Vietnam, in the Champa, until the fourteenth century. They maintained multiple and, usually, violent relations with the Khmers.

16. Banteay: the Khmer word for fortress.

17. Srah (Sanskrit): means basin or pool.

18. Devata (Sanskrit): divinity, designates female figures sculpted on the walls.

19. Gopura: arched entrance door with a tower carved with faces.

20. Apsaras (Sanskrit): celestial beings, consorts of the Gandhavas (celestial beings, singers and musicians), originally water deities who became dancers.

21. Maurice Glaize: architect, restorer and curator of the Angkor temples. He wrote the first major work analysing these buildings, the *Guides des Monuments d'Angkor*, published in 1944 in Saigon and reprinted several times since.

22. Angkor: the Khmer word that means city or capital.

23. Phnom Kulen is consider by Khmers to be the most sacred mountain. It is a widely visited pilgrimage site. The small temple on the mountaintop houses an immense reclining Buddha, which is carved directly into the sandstone.

24. Srei: the Khmer word for woman or beauty.

25. Anastylosis: a restoration technique for a ruined structure based on using the elements found on the site. The discreet and necessary use of new stone replacement materials is allowed if the old elements cannot be restored without them.

26. Spean: the Khmer word for bridge.

27. Linga: stylized phallic image, symbol of the God Shiva and also the pillar that supports the world.

28. Sangkum Reastr Niyum: Popular Socialist Assembly. The national movement headed by King Sihanouk in the 1950s and 1960s.

29. Durga (Sanskrit): a fierce-looking Goddess and one of Shiva's wives. The word also means inaccessible in Khmer.

30. Roland Coignard: trained as a sculptor, he has worked in restoration since 1967. He was particularly interested in new technologies in the study and restoration of stone. Starting in 1995, he made several working trips to Cambodia, where he created restoration workshops with his son, complete with modern equipment and resources for researching and restoring artwork.

31. Kreung: one of the many ethnic tribes, constituting a linguistic minority, in Cambodia. They are located in the country's mountainous north-east. Some 60,000 to 70,000 people live a precarious existence, outside of Khmer society.

32. Annam: former name for Vietnam. The people were called Annamites.

33. Baray: a reservoir that is not dug down, but holds water within strong dikes. They are rectangular and of different size. The largest is the western baray of Angkor.

34. Baphuon: the Baphuon is a pyramidal representation of the mythical Mount Meru. Constructed by Udaya-dityavarman II, it marks the centre of the city that preceded Angkor Thom.

35. Barang: the Khmer word for foreigner.

36. Preah: the Khmer word for saint or sacred.

Bibliography

BIZOT, François, *Le Portail,* Paris, La Table Ronde, 2000.

CHANDLER, David P., *Pol Pot, frère numéro un,* Paris, Plon, 1993.

DAGENS, Bruno, *Angkor, la forêt de pierre,* Paris, Gallimard, coll. «Découvertes», 1989.

DELVERT, Jean, *Le Cambodge,* Paris, Presses universitaires de France, coll. «Que sais-je ?», 1998.

GARNIER, Francis, *Expédition Mékong (1866-1868),* Paris, L'Illustration, 1870-1871.

ENGELMANN, Francis, *L'Indochine à la Belle Époque (1870-1914),* Paris, ASA Editions, coll. «Images d'autrefois», 2001.

GITEAU, Madeleine, *Histoire d'Angkor,* Paris, Kaïlash, coll. «Civilisations & Sociétés», 1999.

GLAIZE, Maurice, *Angkor,* Paris, J. Maisonneuve, 1944.

GROSLIER, Bernard-Philippe, *Indochine,* Paris, Albin Michel, coll. «Carrefour des arts», 1960.

GROSLIER, George, *Le Retour à l'argile,* Paris, Kaïlash, 1996.

GROSLIER, George, *La Route du plus fort,* Paris, Kaïlash, 1997.

JACQUES, Claude, **HELD,** Suzanne, *Angkor, vision de palais divins,* Paris, Hermé, 1997.

JACQUES, Claude, **FREEMAN,** Michael, *Angkor, cité khmère,* Genève, Olizane, 1999.

JARRY, Isabelle, **GELLIE,** Yves, *La Pluie des mangues. Angkor, histoires contemporaines du Cambodge,* Paris, Marval, 1997.

LOTI, Pierre, *Voyages (1872-1913),* Paris, Robert Laffont, coll. « Bouquins », 1991.

LY, Claire, *Revenue de l'enfer,* Paris, Éditions de l'Atelier, 2002.

NEVEU, Roland, *Cambodia, the Years of Turmoil,* Bangkok, Asia Horizons, 2000.

PONCAR, Jaro, *Angkor Revisited,* Cologne, Jaro Poncar Publishing, 2000.

PONCHAUD, François, *Cambodge, année zéro,* Paris, Julliard, 1977.

RAY, Nick, *Cambodge,* Paris, Lonely Planet Publications, 2003.

RIBOUD, Marc, *Angkor, sérénité bouddhique,* Paris, Imprimerie nationale, 1992.

SISAVANG, Sor, *L'Enfant de la rizière rouge,* Paris, Fayard, coll. «Les Enfants du fleuve», 1990.

STANDEN, Mark, *Voyage à travers Angkor,* Bangkok, Mark Standen Publishing, 1997.

STIERLIN, Henri, *Angkor,* Fribourg, Office du Livre, coll. «Architecture universelle», 1970.

TCHEOU TA-KOUAN, *Mémoires sur les coutumes du Cambodge* (traduction de Paul Pelliot), Paris, J. Maisonneuve, 1951.

THIERRY, Solange, *Les Khmers,* Paris, Kaïlash, 1996.

ZÉPHYR, Thierry, *L'Empire des rois khmers,* Paris, Gallimard, coll. «Découvertes»/ Réunion des musées nationaux, 1997.

ZÉPHYR, Thierry, **TETTONI,** Luca, *Angkor, a Tour of the Monuments,* Paris, Archipelago Press, 2003.

Phnom Penh, développement urbain et patrimoine, Paris, Ministère de la Culture, Atelier parisien d'urbanisme, 1990.

2$ CAMBODGE

LES 3 MOUSTIQUAIRES

ស្លូម អរគុណ